Work

Work

HOW TO FIND JOY AND MEANING IN EACH HOUR OF THE DAY

PARALLAX
PRESS
Berkeley, California

Parallax Press
P.O. Box 7355
Berkeley, California 94707
www.parallax.org

Parallax Press is the publishing division
of Unified Buddhist Church
Printed in The United States of America

100% Recycled Content

Edited by Rachel Neumann
Cover and text design by Jess Morphew
Front cover art by Dimitri Vervitsiotis / Digital Vision /
Getty Images

Library of Congress Cataloging-in-Publication Data
Nhat Hanh, Thich.
Work : how to find joy and meaning in each hour of the day
/ Thich Nhat Hanh. -- First edition.
     pages cm
  ISBN 978-1-937006-20-4 (pbk.)
  1. Religious life--Buddhism. I. Title.
BQ9800.T5392N454854 2012
294.3'444--dc23
                                        2012032588

1 2 3 4 5 / 16 15 14 13 12

Contents

CHAPTER FOUR

Coming Home | 71

the art of mindful living and working

THE WAY WE LIVE OUR LIVES and the way we earn our living is crucial to our joy and happiness. Almost half of our life is spent at work, but just how do we spend this time? The work we do is an expression of our entire being. Our work can be a wonderful means for us to express our deepest aspirations, and can be a source of great nourishment, peace, joy, transformation, and healing. Conversely, the work we do and the way we do it can also cause a lot of suffering. What we do with our lives and whether we are mindful or not determines how much peace and joy we create. If we bring our awareness to every moment, if we practice mindfulness in everything we do, our work can help us realize our ideal of living in harmony with others and of cultivating understanding and compassion.

We live in a time and place where it is not easy to find a job. We know, however, that our well-being depends not just on having a source of income, but on having a job in which we can cultivate joy and happiness, a job which is not harmful to humans, animals, plants, or the Earth. Ideally, we are able to find a job and work in such a way that our work is of benefit to the Earth and to all living beings.

No matter what your job is, there is a lot you can do toward helping others and creating a happy work environment, a place where you can work in joy and harmony, without stress and tension. The practices of mindful breathing, mindful sitting, mindful eating, and mindful walking can all contribute to a positive and stress-free environment at work. Learning the art of stopping, of releasing tension, of using loving speech and deep listening, and sharing this practice with others can have a huge impact on our own enjoyment at work and on our company's culture. When we know how to take care of our strong emotions and to establish good relationships at work, communication improves, stress is reduced, and our work becomes much more pleasant. This is a huge benefit not only to ourselves, but also to those we work with, to our loved ones, our families, and the whole of society.

The Energy of Mindfulness

Mindfulness is the act of bringing one's full attention to what is happening in the present moment. We bring our minds back to our bodies, and come home to the present moment. It begins with mindful awareness of our breathing: our in-breath and out-breath. Mindfulness is the kind of energy that helps us to be fully present, to live life in the here and now. Every one of us can generate the energy of mindfulness. When you breathe in and out, focusing on the air moving in and out of your body, this is called mindful breathing. When you drink a glass of water or a cup of tea, focusing all your attention on drinking and not thinking of anything else, this is called mindful drinking. When you walk and focus your awareness on your body, your breathing, your feet, and the steps you make, this is called mindful walking.

Bringing our attention first to our breathing, we are able to unite body and mind and arrive fully in the present moment. From this place, we can be more aware of everything that's happening in the present moment and see it with fresh eyes, without being caught in the past or carried away by worries about the future. You know that the future is just a notion. The future is made of only one substance, and that is the present moment. If you take good care of the present, there is no need to worry about the future. By taking care of the present you are doing everything you can to assure a good future. We should live the present moment in such a way that peace and joy are possible in the here and the now—that love and understanding are possible. That is the best thing we can do for the future.

Every ordinary act can be transformed into an act of mindfulness: brushing your teeth, washing the dishes, walking, eating, drinking, or working. And of course mindfulness is not just mindfulness of positive things. When joy manifests, we practice mindfulness of joy. But when anger manifests, we practice mindfulness of anger. Whatever strong emotion arises, if we learn to practice mindfulness of that emotion, acknowledging the emotion and not suppressing it or acting on it, then transformation occurs and we are able to find more joy, peace, and awareness.

You may think you don't have time to practice mindfulness, that your workday is so full and you are too busy to practice being mindful. You may think mindfulness is something you can only practice when you have time, like when you're on vacation or outside enjoying nature. But we can practice mindfulness anywhere, anytime—at home or at work, even during our very busy workday. We don't need to set time apart in order to practice. It takes only a few breaths to generate the energy of mindfulness and to bring us back to the present moment.

We can practice all day long and get the benefit of our practice straight away. Sitting on the bus, driving the car, taking a shower, cooking breakfast—we can enjoy doing all these things. We can't say, "I have no time to practice." No. We have plenty of time. This is very important to realize. When you practice mindfulness and generate peace and joy, you become an instrument of peace, bringing peace and joy to yourself and to others.

When we come home to the present moment, and let go of thoughts about the past or the future, this is called stopping. We practice stopping in order to be present for ourselves and for the world around us. When we learn to stop, we begin to see, and when we see, we understand. In this way, we can generate understanding, compassion, peace, and happiness. In order to be fully present for our work, for our coworkers, for our friends and family, we need to learn the art of stopping. Until we stop and notice what is happening in the present moment, we cannot generate joy, awareness, or compassion.

I know a man who pays close attention to walking with awareness between business appointments. He walks mindfully, aware of his in-breath and his out-breath, as he walks between office buildings in downtown Denver. Passersby smile at him because he seems so calm amidst all the rushing people. He says that his meetings, even with difficult people, have become a lot easier and more pleasant since he started this practice.

Home and Work Are Connected

The manner in which you get ready for work, go to work, and the way you are while you are there affects not only those you work with, but also the quality of your work. Everything we do in our lives has an effect on our work. I, myself, am a poet but I love working in the garden growing vegetables. One day an American scholar said to me, "Don't waste your time gardening and growing lettuce. You should write more poems instead; anyone can grow lettuce." That is not my way of thinking. I know very well that if I do not grow lettuce, I cannot write poems. The two are interrelated. Eating breakfast mindfully, washing the dishes, and growing lettuce in mindfulness are essential for me to be able to write poetry well. The way someone washes the dishes reveals the quality of his or her poetry. Similarly, the more awareness and mindfulness we bring to all our daily actions, including our work, the better our work will be.

Our personal lives are not separate from our working lives. Our inability to be mindful, to bring our full attention to what we're doing in our everyday lives, has both personal and professional costs. To understand what's happening to us at work, we need to look at our home lives and our families.

The practice of mindfulness helps us to build a healthy immune system for our family. When a virus penetrates the body of an organism, the organism becomes aware that it has been invaded and produces antibodies in order to resist the invader. The immune system is an agent of protection. If there are not enough antibodies to combat the virus, the immune system quickly produces more in order to cope with the invasion and sustain itself. In this way, we can say that the immune system is a reflection of the body's mindful awareness. Similarly, the more mindfulness we produce, the more we can protect and take care of ourselves.

A family is a living organism that has the capacity to protect and heal itself. Suppose your child is suffering. If your child doesn't feel she's receiving enough attention or that anyone is listening to her, she'll try to deal with her problems on her own. Yet because children often don't know how to deal with their suffering, they may try to ignore it, cover it up, or disguise it with unhealthy behavior. Unresolved suffering can affect the whole family. If a child is not happy, the parents or brothers and sisters cannot be happy either. If we can give mindful attention to our child's suffering, acknowledge it, and tend to it, this will help the child to resolve her problems and heal her pain, which will benefit the entire family.

Awareness of suffering and finding ways to help relieve it in our home life will help us be more able to understand and deal with difficult situations that arise at work, particularly if we are in high-stress occupations. We need to know how to handle our own suffering in order to be able to understand others. Our work environment is like a living organism, too. If we bring our stress from home into our work, that stress can be like an infection. Similarly, if we bring mindfulness from home to work, our mindful presence can make our work environment a healthier and happier place for everyone.

We may like to ask ourselves whether we know how to produce a feeling of joy, or if we know how to relax and enjoy eating lunch, or whether we breathe before picking up the phone or before going into a difficult meeting. These questions are very practical and very important. The way we get dressed, brush our teeth, or eat our breakfast in the morning is also important. If we practice mindfulness in these small daily actions, we will know how to enjoy our day, how to let go of tension at work and how to reduce stress. The practice of mindfulness can help us to cultivate more awareness and joy in our lives and in our work.

CHAPTER TWO

beginning
the day

Waking Up

When we wake up in the morning, the first thing we can do is to be aware of the gift that life is offering us. We have a gift of twenty-four hours. We can become aware that we are awake, aware of our breath, aware of the sun and the sky outside, and aware of being alive. We can feel grateful for this. We can say to ourselves,

> *Waking up, I see the blue sky.*
> *I join my palms in gratitude.*

Feeling grateful for what we already have, being aware that we have more than enough conditions for happiness in the present moment is very important. It is good to start the day with this sort of awareness.

Setting Your Intention

When you get up, instead of rushing to get ready for work, you can think about how you want to live your day. Taking a few moments to clarify your aspirations or intentions for the day helps you stay open to whatever is happening and helps you remember that this is a brand-new day, a new beginning, and that you can choose to live the day with mindfulness and compassion.

We all have to look into ourselves to identify our deepest desires and aspirations. Our deepest desire is a source of nourishment, giving us the fuel and energy to live. If our deepest desire is to bring joy to the world, to help people suffer less, to help them transform their suffering and bring peace into their lives, then that is a wholesome kind of nourishment which will give us a lot of energy. If our deepest desire is to take revenge, kill, or destroy, then that is a poison and it will cause us a lot of suffering, and others as well.

You can express your aspiration with a morning *gatha*. A gatha is a small poem that's recited in combination with mindful breathing to deepen your awareness. The following gatha can help you to strengthen your resolve to go through the day in mindfulness.

> *Waking up this morning, I smile.*
> *Twenty-four brand-new hours are before me.*
> *I vow to live fully each moment*
> *and to look at all beings with eyes of compassion.*

We have twenty-four brand-new hours ahead of us. Life comes to our door. We can live these twenty-four hours fully, in mindfulness, in awareness. That is a huge and very precious gift of life: a new day. I vow to go through it in mindfulness. I will not waste this day. I will not spoil it. I will know how to make good use of it, whether at home or at work. No matter where I am or what I'm doing, I'll know how to profit from it, using all my wisdom and all my skill.

Reciting gathas is one way to help us dwell in the present moment and to become deeply aware of the action we are engaged in. When we focus our minds on a gatha, we return to ourselves and become more aware of what we are doing.

As exercises in both meditation and poetry, gathas are a key part of the Zen tradition. When you memorize a gatha, it will come to you quite naturally when you're doing the related activity. You can print these poems out and put them where you can see them when you first wake up in the morning or throughout the day. Or you can keep them with you on a small piece of paper so you can read them anytime. Drinking a cup of tea in the early morning, you might like to recite:

> *Sitting peacefully, I smile.*
> *The new day begins.*
> *I make a vow to live deeply, mindfully.*

Getting Dressed

Getting dressed is another opportunity to practice preparing for our day in mindfulness and to change the way we normally go through our busy workday. Often, we get dressed without considering what we're doing. We're on automatic pilot. When I was a novice monk, I learned to recite this gatha every time I put on my monk's robe to help me be more aware of my actions:

> *Putting on the monk's robe,*
> *My heart is at ease.*
> *I live a life of freedom,*
> *bringing joy to the world.*

You can also use the time of getting dressed as an opportunity to remember your aspirations—your good intentions for the day—by reciting a gatha. I wrote the following version of the above gatha, which goes well not just with monk's robes but with any kind of clothing:

Putting on these clothes,
I am grateful to those who made them
and for the materials from which they were made.
I wish everyone could have enough to wear.

Even if you are not a monk or a nun and do not wear robes, you may like to think of your clothing as a bodhisattva's robe. A bodhisattva (Sanskrit) is an awakened or enlightened being. A bodhisattva is someone who has happiness, peace, awakening, understanding and love. Any living being who has these qualities can be called a bodhisattva. We can use our morning ritual of getting dressed to remind us of our aspiration to live every moment of our daily lives like a bodhisattva: with peace, love, gratitude, understanding, awareness, and freedom.

Brushing Your Teeth

How much time do you spend brushing your teeth? At least one minute, maybe two? You have these two minutes to brush your teeth in such a way that freedom and joy become possible, without being carried away by concerns about what you'll do when you've finished. Consider paying attention to what you're doing while you're brushing your teeth. For example, you could say, "I am standing here, brushing my teeth. I have toothpaste, a toothbrush. I am happy I still have teeth to brush. My practice is to be alive, to be free, and to enjoy brushing my teeth." Don't allow yourself to be caught in the past or carried away by worries about the future. Don't hurry. You can enjoy brushing your teeth. This practice is the practice of freedom. If freedom is there, brushing your teeth will be very enjoyable.

While you're brushing your teeth, you might like to recite

the following gatha to remind you of your desire to use loving speech and cultivate good communication with others during the day:

> *Brushing my teeth and rinsing my mouth,*
> *I vow to speak purely and lovingly.*
> *When my mouth is fragrant with right speech,*
> *a flower blooms in the garden of my heart.*

Breakfast

Many people rush in the morning and don't have time to eat breakfast. They grab something to eat on their way to work, and eat it in the car, on the train, or at their desk when they arrive at work. But breakfast isn't just about supplying your body with food—it's a chance to enjoy eating, to nourish yourself, and to practice cultivating gratitude and awareness. When you take the time at home to prepare your breakfast, this time of making breakfast becomes a time of practice. You do everything as you normally do, but you breathe in and out mindfully while doing so, following your breath and becoming aware of your breath moving into and out of the body. When you practice in your kitchen like this, your kitchen becomes a meditation hall.

When you eat your breakfast, even if it's just a small bite early in the morning, eat in such a way that freedom is possible. You can chew every morsel of your breakfast in mindfulness, with joy and freedom. While eating, don't think about what you have to do next or all the things you have to do that day. Your practice is to just be there for your breakfast. Your breakfast is there for you; you have to be there for your breakfast. In this way you can touch deeply what is right in front of you. What is there is the awareness of you yourself, and the fact that you are still alive. What is there is your breakfast, a gift of the earth and the sky. What is there may also include your friends or your family, sitting and enjoying their breakfast together with you.

When I hold a piece of bread, I like to look at it and smile to it. The piece of bread is an ambassador of the cosmos, offering nourishment and support. Looking deeply into the piece of bread, I see the sunshine, the clouds, and Mother Earth. Without the sunshine, without water, without soil, wheat can't grow. Without the clouds, there would be no rain for the wheat crops. Without Mother Earth supporting all life, nothing could grow at all. That's why the piece of bread that I hold in my hand is a true wonder of life. And it's there for us, so we have to be there for it as well. Eat with gratitude. When you put a piece of bread into your mouth, chew only your bread and not your projects, worries, fears, or anger. This is the practice of mindfulness. You chew mindfully and you know that you're chewing the bread, the wonderful nourishment of life. This brings you freedom and joy. Eat every morsel of your breakfast like that, not allowing yourself to be pulled away from the experience of eating.

In Plum Village, the meditation and practice center in the southwest of France where I live, we take a moment before we eat to contemplate our food. Even if we only have a very short time to eat, taking a moment to first contemplate our food makes it much more enjoyable when we eat it. Here are the Five Contemplations we use, in case you would like to keep them by your table and use them as well.

The Five Contemplations

1. This food is a gift of the whole universe, the earth, the sky, numerous living beings and much hard and loving work.
2. May we eat with mindfulness and gratitude so as to be worthy to receive this food.
3. May we recognize and transform unwholesome mental formations, especially our greed, and learn to eat in moderation.
4. May we keep our compassion alive by eating in such a way that we reduce the suffering of living beings, preserve our planet, and reverse the effects of global warming.
5. We accept this food so that we may nurture our brotherhood and sisterhood, build our Sangha, and nourish our ideal of serving all living beings.

Going Out the Door

When you go to work in the morning, you have a wonderful opportunity to become aware of the whole world around you. You open the door and go out into the fresh air. Here is your chance to be in touch with the earth, the air, and the sky. Your very first step out the door can already be a step in freedom. You don't have to go to a meditation hall and open the door to be in the world of meditation. Every step on the earth can bring us a lot of happiness, peace, and freedom.

The same is true for our breathing. If we know how to breathe mindfully, aware of our in-breath and out-breath, every breath will bring us happiness. People who have asthma or who have difficulty breathing understand what a precious gift it is to be able to breathe in and out with ease. If you can take a smooth breath, then savor each breath. Don't waste a moment. Every breath brings happiness; every step brings freedom. When we walk and breathe like that, we don't feel trapped in our daily routine or by going to work. Instead, we feel free and we're grateful for our lives.

In the Jataka Tales, one of the earliest collections of Buddhist literature, we can read about the former lives of the Buddha. In these stories, the Buddha appears in different manifestations, sometimes as a deer, a monkey, a rock, or even a mango tree. In each of these manifestations, whether animal, plant, or mineral, we can see a bodhisattva, a being of great compassion. When we go out our front door and take our first steps on the earth, even if it's covered in concrete, we can still see and feel nature all around us, and we can recognize that nature is also a bodhisattva. When we look deeply at a tree, we can see that the tree offers its beauty to us, and that it nourishes and sustains life. Its leaves help clean the air we breathe and it provides a safe place of refuge for so many birds. There are bodhisattvas all around us—our entire planet Earth is a bodhisattva. It carries us very solidly. It's very patient and doesn't discriminate. No matter what we throw on the earth, it embraces and accepts it without discrimination. Whether we throw fragrant flowers or perfumed oil on the earth, or whether we throw urine, excrement, or other impure substances, the earth can absorb and transform all of these things. It has a great capacity to be patient and to endure. It offers up so much that nourishes us and supports all life. It gives us water; it gives us air to breathe and food to eat. It is a true bodhisattva. Every time we walk out the door, even if we're just on the way to our car to go to work, we can take the time to notice that the great Earth bodhisattva is all around us, nourishing and sustaining us.

Arriving at Work

Perhaps you manage to spend the morning in a lovely, relaxed, and mindful way, but as soon as you start on your way to work, it's all forgotten! This can easily happen if you drive to work in rush-hour traffic. But if you are on a train or a bus, you have the wonderful opportunity to just sit there and be aware of your in-breath and your out-breath. You can even close your eyes or keep them lowered if it helps you focus on your breathing.

If you drive to work, take a moment when you get into the car, before putting the key in the ignition, to remember your intention to be calm, relaxed, and mindful while driving, and not stressed or in a hurry.

> *Before starting the car,*
> *I know where I'm going.*
> *The car and I are one.*
> *If the car goes fast, I go fast.*

This awareness can help you to enjoy the entire trip. Use every red light or stop sign as an opportunity to take a mindful breath and return to the present moment. You may be used to thinking of the red light as your enemy, preventing you from achieving your goal of getting to work on time. But in fact the red light is your friend, helping you resist the urge to rush, and calling you back to the here and now.

The next time you are caught in traffic, whether on the highway or in the middle of the city, don't fight. Just accept it. It's useless to fight. Sit back and smile to yourself. Know that you're alive and that the present moment is the only moment of life available to you. Don't waste it. Know that this moment has the potential to be a wonderful one.

When you drive to and from work in this way, without thinking of your destination or of what you're going to do when you arrive, you can enjoy every moment of driving. Before I begin my work of teaching for the day, I don't worry about what questions people might ask me or how I might answer them. Instead, from my room to the place where I teach, I enjoy every step and every breath fully, and I live each moment of my walk deeply. When I arrive, I feel fresh and ready to offer answers to any questions I may be asked.

If you arrive at work having practiced mindfulness while getting ready at home as well as on your way to work, you will arrive in a very different way than in the past—happier and more relaxed. You may find you now think about your work and coworkers differently, and you may find unexpected sources of satisfaction and joy.

CHAPTER THREE

mindfulness at work

WE'RE USED TO MAKING A DISTINCTION between "work time" and "free time." But this way of thinking lessens our joy and our success at work. We can work in such a way that we realize we have a lot of choices in what we do and how we do it. We can work in such a way that we find opportunities for joy, and we don't get stuck in the habit of suffering from pressure or stress. When we practice mindfulness, we can practice enjoying working, typing, planning, organizing, having meetings, dealing with clients, or any of the other activities we do in what we usually call our "workday." If we put all our heart and mind into everything we do, freedom and joy become possible.

We spend so much time at work; we need to make sure we enjoy it. Any job can be enjoyable if we do it in the right spirit, with mindfulness, with awareness, and with the aim of helping living beings. Whether we work in a factory, in a restaurant, or in an office, whether we're in a helping profession or not, if we practice mindfulness our work can be enjoyable and can bring great benefit to ourselves and to others.

We have the tendency to rush, to try to finish what we're doing quickly. This has become a habit. With mindfulness of breathing, you can recognize this habit. Mindfulness helps you to stop and not be carried away by the habit of rushing. If we know how to live every moment of our daily lives, we won't become victims of stress. While eating breakfast, washing the dishes, going to work, we enjoy eating breakfast, washing the dishes, and going to work.

Our work time can bring us pleasure if we handle it in the right way. There's a way to not feel pressure, and to really enjoy the work we do. In Plum Village, we do a lot of things: we welcome guests throughout the year and offer numerous retreats, at home as well as in many different countries around the world. Like many businesses, we, too, want to succeed in our work. But we learn how to work so that we don't become victims of pressure or stress. We enjoy gardening, cleaning, cooking, and washing the dishes—we consider these things as equally important as other kinds of work. We put all our hearts and minds into everything we do and we do it in such a way that freedom, joy, brotherhood and sisterhood are possible at every moment.

Mindful Breathing

Mindful breathing—being aware of our in-breath and our out-breath and following the breath as it moves in and out of the body—brings about a feeling of peace and harmony. We benefit from this energy of peace and harmony in our breathing as it penetrates into our bodies. Whether we're lying down, sitting, or standing, the stress, conflict, and tension in the body and mind will slowly be released by our practice of mindful breathing.

We would all like to have the time to sit and appreciate the stillness that comes from doing nothing. But if we were given the time, would we really be able to sit still and enjoy being quiet? Many of us have this problem. We complain that we don't have the time to rest, to enjoy just being, but this is because we are used to always doing something. We have no capacity to rest and do nothing. Even if we have a rare moment of quiet at our desks, we talk on the phone or browse the internet. We are workaholics. We always need to be doing something.

If you can find a moment to sit, wherever you are, stay there and enjoy doing nothing. Just enjoy your in-breath and out-breath. Of course, you don't have to be in a sitting position to practice mindful breathing. You might be standing in line to photocopy something at work or waiting to talk with a colleague.

You may be out at lunch or waiting to get a cup of tea or coffee. You can practice mindful breathing anywhere and focus on enjoying yourself and the presence of the people around you.

When you breathe in, if you bring your full attention to your in-breath, you become your in-breath. When you're mindful of your in-breath and concentrated on it, you and your in-breath become one. Don't think that this is something difficult or tiring to do. Breathing in can be very enjoyable. When you breathe in, you can appreciate the fact that you are still alive. Breath is the essence of life; without breath, you would be nothing but a dead body. To be aware of your vitality through breathing can bring immense joy. If you're used to the practice, this awareness is present whenever you breathe. You don't have to force the breath. You allow yourself to breathe in naturally. Don't try to struggle with your in-breath. Just let it be the way it is—whether it is short or long, fast or slow, deep or shallow. Just become aware of it. As you breathe, you can say to yourself:

> *Breathing in, I am aware of my in-breath.*
> *Breathing out, I am aware of my out-breath.*
> *Breathing in, I am aware of my body.*
> *Breathing out, I release the tension in my body.*

Don't interfere with your breath. Just become aware of it and follow the whole length of the in-breath and out-breath. During the time you become aware of your in- and out-breath, you naturally stop your thinking. Stopping your thoughts is very helpful. Focusing on your breathing can help you to stop worrying about the troubles of the past or the uncertainty of the future. If you're caught in your thinking all the time, you get tired and aren't capable of being truly present. Don't think about your projects—you won't solve your problems by thinking. Our practice is non-thinking. This is the secret of success. Don't try to find solutions with your thinking mind. You just plant a seed and let it grow underground. The solution will come to you when it's ripe. The time when you're not working can be very productive if you know how to focus on the present moment. If you know how to do this, you won't become a victim of anxiety or stress, or suffer from depression.

You can stop your train of thoughts quite naturally if you focus your attention fully on your in- and out-breath. After only a few in- and out-breaths, the quality of your breathing will improve. Your breath will become deeper, slower, more harmonious and peaceful, whether you're lying down, sitting, or walking. It takes only a few breaths made in mindfulness to become free, to relax, and to release the tension in the body and mind.

Being fully aware of our breathing like this is the practice of mindfulness. It allows us to see deeply what is here and now and to get in touch with the wonders of life so that we will be strong and lucid enough to handle the difficult situations we encounter at work.

Space to Breathe

It may be helpful to have a special area at work that reminds you to breathe. You may like to arrange a beautiful, calm, and relaxing space in one part of your office or it may just be a corner of your desk that you keep clean except for a small bell or a flower. It may help you to focus on your mindful breathing to look at the bell or the flower. If you have colleagues who are interested in joining you in the practice of mindful breathing, you can find an appropriate area, for example a nice place outside, in the room where you take breaks, or even in someone's office, to set up a calm, beautiful, and relaxing space where you can sit together and enjoy coming back to your breathing.

A Bell of Mindfulness

You might like to get a small Japanese-style bell, called a mini-bell, and bring it to work with you. You can put it in your bag or keep it on your desk and when you need a breathing break you can invite the bell to "wake up," by tapping it lightly on the rim with the inviter. Then take a slow breath in and out before inviting the bell to sound fully. Continue to breathe peacefully while you enjoy listening to the beautiful sound. When we hear the sound of the bell, we're reminded to come home to ourselves, to come back to our breathing, and to touch life deeply in the present moment. This is called a bell of mindfulness, because its sound immediately brings us back to ourselves, uniting body and mind by means of the breath. This is very healing. When the atmosphere isn't very calm or pleasant at work, you can use the bell in order to come back to yourself, and to breathe quietly and mindfully for a few minutes. You'll feel much better afterward and the atmosphere will be transformed.

In Plum Village, many of the monks and nuns have programmed a bell of mindfulness to sound on their computers every fifteen minutes, reminding them to take a break from their work and come back to themselves, to come home to the body and enjoy their breathing. Breathing in and out three times is enough to release tension in the body and mind. During these few moments, the body becomes the only object of your mind. You stop all other thinking, all your worries about the past or the future. This brings us freedom. Freedom is possible in just a few breaths.

Anything in your daily life can be your bell of mindfulness—the phone ringing, a digital watch sounding the hour or half-hour, a clock chiming, church bells ringing, the sound the elevator makes when it arrives at your floor, a stop sign, a red traffic light. You can use all of these of these as an opportunity to stop thinking, to come back to your breathing and your body, and to enjoy a few moments of peace and relaxation in the present moment.

Sitting

Many of us spend a lot of our workday sitting. But what is the quality of our sitting? Do we enjoy sitting? We could stop working every hour or so for a few minutes and instead of sitting to do our work, we could sit just for the sake of sitting. We could sit in order to enjoy the act of sitting and breathing and for no other purpose. We can do this without changing very much, and without anyone noticing what we're doing,

While I was a novice monk practicing in a temple called Hai Duc in Vietnam, I once observed an old Zen master sitting all alone, not in the mediation hall but on a traditional low seat. We didn't have tables or chairs at this temple, just flat pieces of wood to sit on. I saw the master sitting there very beautifully and very straight. That image has stayed with me. He was sitting so upright, so peacefully and naturally. I looked at him and realized in my heart that I had a longing to sit like that. I, too, wanted to be able to sit in such a way—without effort, without any apparent purpose. Sitting like that would bring me happiness. I wouldn't need to do anything. I wouldn't need to say anything. I would just sit.

Sitting for the Sake of Sitting

How can we sit like that, too? What is the purpose of sitting like that? That monk wasn't sitting there for any purpose. He was just sitting for the sake of sitting, just to enjoy the sitting. If you ask children why they eat chocolate, most would just say it's because they enjoy eating chocolate; they wouldn't be able to give you a rational explanation. Standing in a beautiful spot outside can be like this as well. If someone asks me why I'm just standing in a particular spot, what should I tell them? I usually don't have a purpose or a reason; I'm standing just to stand. I enjoy standing in that beautiful place. There's no goal in standing there and there's no goal in eating chocolate either. We stand in a place or we eat chocolate because we like it.

So the next time when you're sitting at work, you can take a break and sit like that—sit like the Buddha. Sit with your back straight, but not rigid. Allow the air to flow freely into your body and feel the movement of your abdomen in and out. When your spine is straight and you feel that you're upright, you can relax your whole body. You don't need to become a full-time Buddha. You don't need to be fully enlightened. A part-time Buddha is good enough. The only thing you need is the freedom of the present moment. You aren't pulled away by the past or the future, nor are you pulled away by your afflictions of anger, worry, or jealousy. With your whole body and mind, you can sit like a free person.

When we sit, we sit to be happy. We sit to have the awareness that we are here, alive, surrounded by a wonderful world, which is also inside of us. If we sit like that, we are in touch with the wonders of life inside us and around us, and we already have happiness. Even if we're indoors, even if it's daytime, we still know that high above our heads there are so many stars. There is the Milky Way, our galaxy of stars, a river made up of trillions of stars. We're sitting on a planet, a very beautiful planet, which is revolving in the galaxy. If we sit and we can clearly see the wonders of our planet Earth and of the universe, what else do we need to sit for? When we sit like that, we have awareness. We can embrace the whole world, from the past to the future. If at that moment a colleague were to walk by your office or your desk while you were sitting like this, what would they see? They would just see you sitting peacefully, your heart and mind at peace, a smile on your face.

Mindful Walking

Although your job may require you to spend most of your day sitting, there are always opportunities to walk, even if it's just from the parking lot to your office, from one office to another, or to the restroom. When you walk with mindfulness, connecting your walking and your breathing, and focusing your awareness on the soles of your feet, every step becomes nourishing and healing. Every step can bring you joy. You need this joy in order to continue to do your work well. Without this kind of nourishment, how can you continue? If you know the art of mindful walking, then the times at work when you can walk with ease and awareness will be something that you'll start looking forward to and this can make your whole workday more enjoyable.

Every one of us has the tendency to run instead of walk. We have been running all our lives, and we even continue to run into the future, where we think we will find happiness. We have inherited the habit of running from our parents and ancestors. Once we've learned to recognize our habit of running, we can use mindful breathing to slow down our steps, and simply smile at this habit and say: "Hello, my dear old friend, I know you are there." You don't have to fight your desire to walk quickly. There is no fighting in this practice. There is only recognition and awareness of what is going on.

If you are a health-care professional—a doctor, a nurse, a therapist, a social worker, or an emergency medical technician— the practice of walking meditation can be particularly helpful as your job involves dealing with many people who are ill and suffering. Walking with mindfulness can give you the strength and peace of mind you need to do this kind of work by helping you to get in touch with the wonders of life and enabling you to cultivate peace and joy within yourself.

We're in the habit of not giving ourselves enough time to walk. If we have a meeting, we rush to get there, with no time to practice walking meditation on the way. Suppose you need to go to the airport. You think that you have enough time to linger and wait until the last minute before leaving your house or office. But there may be heavy traffic, you'll arrive late, or you'll have to rush. You can always plan so that you have plenty of time to walk as a free person in the airport. Give yourself an extra hour in order to have the pleasure of doing walking meditation at the airport before boarding your plane.

Practicing Walking Meditation

There are two kinds of walking meditation. The first is slow walking. Slow walking is especially helpful for beginners. As you breathe in, you take one step. When you breathe out, you take another step. Bring your full attention to the contact between your foot and the ground. Breathing in, you make one step with your left foot. You can say to yourself: "I have arrived." This is not a declaration; this is a practice. You have to really arrive. "Arrive where?" you may ask. Arrive in the here and now. According to this teaching and practice, life is only available in the here and now. The past has already gone. The future is not yet here. There is only one moment when you can be truly alive, and that is the present moment. When you breathe out, you make another step with your right foot and you say, "I am home." My true home is not in the past, not in the future. My true home is life itself—it is in the here and now. I have arrived at my true home; I feel at ease in my true home. I don't need to run anymore.

Your steps bring you back to the present so that you can touch the wonders of life that are available in the present moment. You have made an appointment with life for the here and now. If you miss the present moment, you miss your appointment with life. Mindful walking is a wonderful way to learn and to train ourselves to live in the here and now. It means being truly alive. If you're lost in the past, or if you're carried away by the future, you're not really living your life. Only by deeply touching the present moment can you touch true life and be truly alive.

When you breathe in and say, "I have arrived," if you feel that you've really arrived, then smile. Smile to yourself a smile of victory. It's very important to arrive, because when you arrive, you don't run anymore. You've stopped running. Many of us continue to run even in our sleep. We can never rest. In our dreams, in our nightmares, we continue to run. That's why we have to train ourselves to stop. Stopping helps us to be in the here and now and to touch the wonders of life for our transformation and healing. "I have arrived, I am home."

This is the first type of walking meditation. Walking slowly can be done anywhere, anytime. You can try walking meditation when you walk across your office or go between offices, when you go to the restroom or walk around the park on your lunch break. Don't think that you have to be a "Buddhist" or understand everything about mindfulness right away. Anyone can practice walking mindfully. All you need is willingness, and you will be able to arrive in the here and now. You may be surprised to find you will start to feel at home wherever you are, even if you are at work!

The second type of walking meditation involves walking a little more quickly, but still maintaining awareness of your footsteps and your breathing, still in touch with the earth beneath your feet, with your breath, and with the world around you.

Breathing in, you may like to take two or three steps and repeat to yourself with each step: "I have arrived, I have arrived, I have arrived." When you breathe out, you may like to make another two or three steps and say: "I am home, I am home, I am home." When I breathe in, I can make two or three steps, and breathing out, three or four steps. I do it very naturally; people may not know that I'm doing mindful walking. I enjoy every step. Walking like this we're inhabited by the energy of mindfulness, which calms us and protects us, keeping us safe and content in the present moment. You can do this when you're walking to the bus stop, to a meeting, or to an appointment. You may like to take a certain distance, one block for example, to practice slow walking. Or you might like to walk from the parking lot to your office every day in this way.

Enjoy every step and touch the wonders of life. Stop all your thinking. You can do this when you're walking with other people, and they may not even notice.

Every time you have five or ten minutes, you can enjoy this practice. Walking from one building to another, you practice mindful walking, and you can enjoy every step. I always enjoy walking. I only have one style of walking: mindful walking. Even if the distance is only one or two feet, I always apply these techniques and enjoy mindful walking.

Eating at Work

Another opportunity to practice mindfulness is when we eat. We often snack at work, just to have something to do. We're bored and want to put something into our mouths. Perhaps we feel stressed, or we're anxious or worried about our work and we want to cover up these unpleasant feelings by eating or drinking something, by consuming something. If you feel this urge, try sitting and breathing mindfully to calm your feelings of worry or restlessness. If you do eat something, think about what you're eating and see if it's nourishing for your body and spirit. In many parts of Asia, since ancient times, no distinction is made between food and medicine—what we eat should be beneficial for our body and mind and should maintain our balance and well-being. When we eat and breathe properly, we nourish our blood, our body, and our spirit. But if we don't eat the right kinds of food, or if we eat too much, it can make us sick in both body and mind. We should select what we eat carefully and chew our food very well.

Even if you manage to choose a healthy snack at work, you can still eat it in an unhealthy manner, for example by continuing to work with one hand while holding your food in the other. Many years ago, I met a young American named Jim who asked me to teach him about the practice of mindfulness. One time when we were together, I offered him a tangerine. Jim accepted the tangerine, but he continued talking about the many projects he was involved in—his work for peace, social justice, and so on. He was eating, but, at the same time, he was thinking and talking. I was there with him as he peeled the tangerine and tossed the sections of it into his mouth, quickly chewing and swallowing.

Finally, I said to him, "Jim, stop!" He looked at me, and I said, "Eat your tangerine." He understood. So he stopped talking, and began to eat much more slowly and mindfully. He separated each of the remaining sections of the tangerine carefully, smelled their beautiful fragrance, put one section at a time into his mouth, and felt the juices surrounding his tongue. Tasting and eating the tangerine this way took several minutes, but he knew that he had enough time to enjoy eating the tangerine. When he finished eating this way, he realized that the tangerine had become real, the eater of the tangerine had become real, and life had also become real in that moment. What is the purpose of eating a tangerine? It's just for eating the tangerine. During the time you eat a tangerine, eating the tangerine is the most important thing in your life.

The next time you have a snack at work, like a tangerine, please put it in the palm of your hand and look at it in a way that makes the tangerine real. You don't need a lot of time to do this, just two or three seconds. Looking at it, you can see a beautiful tree, a blossom, sunshine, and rain, and you can see a tiny fruit forming. You can see the continuation of the sunshine and the rain, and the transformation of the baby fruit into the fully developed tangerine in your hand. You can see the color change from green to orange and you can see the tangerine sweetening. Looking at a tangerine in this way, you will see that everything in the cosmos is in it—the sunshine, rain, clouds, trees, leaves, everything. Peeling the tangerine, smelling it, and tasting it, you can be very happy.

Restroom Meditation

No matter what else you do at work, you probably have to use the restroom. In the United States it is called the restroom, but do you feel restful in your restroom? In France, the word for restroom used to be *le cabinet d'aisance. Aisance* means ease; so it's a place you feel at ease, you feel comfortable. So when you go to the restroom, allow yourself to feel at ease there; enjoy the time you spend in the restroom. Know that your time spent there is no less important than anything else you have to do. The restroom becomes your meditation hall. That's my practice. When I urinate, I allow myself to be entirely with the act of urinating. If you have freedom, then urinating can be very pleasant. You allow yourself to invest one hundred percent of your body and mind in the act of urinating. It can free you. It can be joyful. If you've had the experience of having a urinary tract infection, you know that urinating can be painful. But now you don't have an infection, therefore urinating is very pleasant, restful. Be free during the thirty seconds or so of urinating.

Answering the Phone

You can turn every time you talk on the telephone into a mindfulness practice. Whenever the telephone rings, you can hear it as a bell of mindfulness, reminding you to stop what you're doing and come back to the present moment. Instead of rushing to answer the phone, breathe in and out with awareness three times before answering to make sure you are truly present for whoever is calling you. You stop your thinking and come back to the present moment, recognizing any feelings of stress or irritation you may have. You may like to put your hand on the receiver while breathing to let your coworkers know that you intend to pick up the phone, you're just not in a hurry. This will help them, too, not to feel they are victims of the telephone.

If you want to call someone on the telephone, you might like to recite the following gatha before you dial the number:

> *Words can travel thousands of miles.*
> *May my words create mutual understanding and love.*
> *May they be as beautiful as gems,*
> *as lovely as flowers.*

Releasing Tension

Stress and tension can accumulate in your body, but with intelligence and compassion, you can release tension and help to create the sort of work conditions in which you and those around you can experience more joy and less stress. If you know how to release the tension in your body, if you're able to relax, you can help the other members of your family and the people you work with to be able to do this, too. If you don't know how to release tension and stress in yourself, how can you expect others at work to be able to release the tension in themselves, or to be able to take care of their families? And if their family situations aren't good, how can they be happy and productive at work? So anything you can do for yourself and for your family also helps take care of the people at work, which in turn helps the whole work environment. You can enjoy the practice of total relaxation and share it with others to help them release the tension that has built up inside them, to experience more lightness and joy both at work and at home.

You can practice total relaxation at work every day in order to release tension and regain your freshness. You only need five or ten minutes between scheduled appointments or during your lunch break. This is an opportunity for your body to rest, to heal, and be restored. We relax our body and give attention to each part in turn, and send our love to every cell. We can guide our attention to any part of the body: the head, scalp, brain, eyes, ears, jaw, lungs, heart, liver, the internal organs, digestive system, and any part of the body that needs healing and attention, embracing each part and sending love and gratitude to it as we breathe in and out.

You can help yourself and your colleagues to relax and feel happier by sharing this practice with them. You may like to organize a quiet room where you can practice deep relaxation together.

Total Relaxation

Total relaxation is a practice of letting go. We become aware of parts of the body, our head, limbs, organs, or individual muscle groups, and consciously relax them, proceeding through the body until we're totally relaxed.

Loosen any tight clothing and lie down on your back with your head and spine aligned, your arms slightly away from your body, your palms facing upward, your legs straight. Let your feet fall outward naturally. You can put a small pillow under your neck to support it. You may want to put a cushion, a blanket, or a pillow under your knees so that your lower back can straighten, relaxing the spine more.

Let go of any busy thoughts and allow your body and mind to completely rest for the next ten minutes. This time is just for you. Become aware of your breath as it moves into and out of the body. Notice the gentle rising and falling of the abdomen. Don't try to control the breath, just follow it. Quite naturally your breath will become deeper and slower.

Move your awareness to your toes and feet. Become aware of each toe. Feel the heel resting on the ground. Tense the muscles in the toes and feet and then let them go. Move your awareness to your calves and tighten these muscles, then let go. Do the same with the knees, thighs, hips, and buttocks. Let both legs completely relax. Notice how they start to feel heavier and sink into the ground. You can repeat this process of tightening and relaxing as you move up the body, focusing on different muscle groups. Finish with your head, your jaw, and your eyes. Send your love and gratitude to each part of the body as you move through it, to all your internal organs, and even to each cell.

You may think that you need to return home at the end of a hard day's work before you can relax, but deep relaxation is a practice you can do anytime to release the tension in the body. You don't need to wait. If you're stressed all day and wait until you go home in the evening to finally relax, you may not be able to, because your mind and body will be so wound up.

When you breathe in and come back to your body, you may notice that there's a lot of tension in your body that prevents you from being relaxed, peaceful, and happy. So you become motivated by a desire to do something to help your body suffer less. While breathing in and breathing out, you just allow the tension in your body to be released. You let go. That is the practice of total relaxation.

If you only have a few minutes, you can recite these verses:

Breathing in, I release the tension in my body.
Breathing out, I smile.

Breathing in, I'm aware of my eyes.
Breathing out, I smile to my eyes.

When you generate the energy of mindfulness, you embrace your eyes and smile to them. This is mindfulness of our eyes. You touch one of the conditions for happiness that exists. It's a wonderful thing to have eyes that are still in good condition. A paradise of forms and colors is available to you at any time. You need only to open your eyes.

Breathing in, I'm aware of my heart.
Breathing out, I smile to my heart.

When you use the energy of mindfulness to embrace your heart and smile to it, you see that your heart is still functioning normally, and you feel so grateful. Many people wish they had a heart that functioned normally. It is a basic condition for our well-being, another condition for our happiness. When you hold your heart with the energy of mindfulness, your heart feels warm and comforted. You have neglected your heart for a long time. You think only about other things. You run after things that you believe to be the true conditions for happiness while you forget about your heart.

You even cause trouble for your heart by the way you eat, drink, rest, and work. Every time you light a cigarette, you make your heart suffer. You commit an unfriendly act toward your heart when you drink alcohol. You put a strain on your heart when you work long hours in a stressful job and don't have enough rest. You know that your heart has been working for your well-being for many years, day and night, but because of your lack of mindfulness, you haven't been very kind to your heart. You don't know how to protect the conditions of well-being and happiness within you. But now you can do something for your heart. You can send it your love, embrace it, and thank it for being there.

You can continue to do this practice with other parts of your body, like your liver. Embrace your liver with tenderness, love, and compassion. Generate mindfulness by means of your breathing and hold your liver in mindfulness. When you direct the energy of mindfulness to the part of your body that you're embracing with love and tenderness, you're doing exactly what your body needs. If a part of your body doesn't feel well, you have to spend more time holding it with mindfulness, and smiling to it. You may not have time to give attention to every part of your body in one session, but once or twice each day you can pick at least one part of your body to focus on and practice relaxing.

Whatever the position of the body, whether you're lying, standing, sitting, or walking, you can always release the tension. Sitting on the bus, you can practice breathing and releasing the tension within you. Walking to a meeting, you can allow the tension to be released with each step. You walk like a free person. You enjoy every step you make. You aren't in a hurry any more. When you walk to the bus stop or from the parking lot to your office in mindfulness, you can be releasing tension with each step and you arrive at your office feeling fresh, light, and free.

Finding a Home at Work

In most work situations, we have to work together with others. We may work with other people in a team, in the same office or workspace, or to carry out a project or achieve a particular goal. But each person in the group has their own difficulties and suffering which they bring to work with them. When you come to work ready, happy, fresh, and at peace within yourself, you help your coworkers to do the same. You care about more than just the quality of their work or service, because the quality of the work they do depends very much on the peace and the well-being inside each of them. So you go to work as a bodhisattva, or as a group of bodhisattvas, with the aspiration of helping others to transform and overcome their suffering, bringing peace, harmony, and well-being to your coworkers and to the entire workplace. You create happiness and harmony at work.

Sometimes we feel insecure in our work environment, we don't feel safe, we don't feel accepted, or we're afraid of rejection. However, when we go to the mountains and spend time among the trees and the animals, it seems that they accept us, that we're stepping into a place where we feel accepted. We're not afraid that they'll look at us and judge us. But at work, we're afraid we're not approved of. We're afraid of being ourselves. We try to behave in way that we feel will make us acceptable to people. This is a tragedy.

A flower doesn't have this kind of fear. She grows in the garden with many other kinds of flowers, but she doesn't try to be like any of the other flowers. She accepts herself as she is. Don't try to be someone or something else. If we are born as we are, we don't need to change into something else. We need to learn to accept ourselves as we are. The cosmos has come together and helped us to manifest in this way, and we are beautiful like this. To be beautiful means to be yourself.

The Island of Self

When the Buddha was eighty years old and knew he wasn't going to live much longer, he offered the practice of the "island of self" to his students. He said that there is a safe island within yourself that you can go back to every time you feel afraid, unstable, or in despair. Go home to the island of self inside of you and take refuge in that island and you will be safe. The island of self is just one breath away. With the practice of mindful breathing or mindful walking, we can come home to our island straight away.

Before moving to Plum Village, I used to stay in a hermitage about an hour's drive from Paris. One day I left my hermitage to go for a walk. The morning was very beautiful, so before leaving, I opened all the windows and doors. But at about four in the afternoon, the weather changed; the wind came up, clouds covered the sun, and it started to rain. I knew that I should go home so I practiced mindful walking back to the hermitage. When I arrived, I found my little hermitage in a very bad state. It was dark, cold, and miserable inside the hermitage; it was no longer a pleasant place to be. But I knew what I had to do. The first thing was to close all the doors and windows. The second thing was to make a fire in the wood-burning stove. After that, I lit a kerosene lamp. Then I went to collect all the sheets of paper that had been blown all around the hermitage. When everything had been picked up and put back in its proper place, I sat close to the fireplace and warmed myself by the fire. Now the hermitage had become a cozy, pleasant place to be again. I was safe and comfortable in my hermitage.

This image can illustrate what to do when we feel down or upset in our daily lives. We try hard, but the harder we try, the worse we feel. We say, "It's just not my day." We seem to fail in everything we attempt to do. We try to say or do something to improve the situation, but it doesn't work. This is the time to go back to our hermitage and close all the doors and windows. Go home to yourself by way of your mindful breathing, and recognize the feelings inside. There may be feelings of anger, of fear, of anxiety, or of despair. Whatever feeling is there, recognize it, and embrace it very tenderly.

When a mother hears her baby crying, she stops whatever she's doing and goes directly to the baby. The first thing she does is to pick up the baby and hold her tenderly in her arms. In the baby there is the energy of suffering. In the mother there is the energy of tenderness, which begins to penetrate into the body of the baby. Similarly, your fear is your baby. Your anger is your baby. Your despair is your baby. Your baby needs you to go home and take care of it. Go home to your hermitage, to the island of self right away, and take care of your baby.

The energy of mindfulness is the mother; with the energy of mindfulness you can hold your baby. Mindfulness is an energy you can generate. It is the capacity to be aware of what is going on. It's the heat you can produce by making a fire. The fire, the heat, will transform the cold and misery in your hermitage. Your baby is you; you shouldn't try to suppress the strong emotions or negative feelings you have. Your fear, your anger is you; don't fight it. Don't struggle against your fear, your anger, or your despair. With mindfulness, you can embrace these feelings. If you continue to breathe mindfully, the energy of mindfulness will be generated and will embrace and calm your difficult feelings, like a mother tenderly embracing and calming her crying baby.

Handling Strong Emotions at Work

It's very important to learn how to deal with our strong emotions at work in order to maintain good relations with others, to keep communication open, and not to create a negative or oppressive work atmosphere. There are practices to help us deal with our strong emotions and we all need to learn these practices in good times, before strong emotions arise, so we know what to do when we're faced with this situation.

The first practice is to realize that all emotions are impermanent—they arise, they stay for a while, and they pass. It's very important to stop all our thinking when a strong emotion comes up in us, not fueling the fire with our thoughts. We need to stop straight away and come back to our breathing, practicing deep abdominal breathing. This is the second practice. Immediately withdraw your attention from the person, thing, or situation which you believe to be the cause of your anger or frustration, and return to your body, following your in- and out-breath. Just follow it. You don't need to force it to change; simply bringing your concentration and awareness to your breathing will naturally allow your breathing to become calmer, deeper, and smoother on its own. Don't force the breath to become slower or deeper—just observe it; let it be as it is.

If you're able to bring mindfulness to your breathing in this way, not only will your breathing calm down, but your body and mind will also become calmer. A good practitioner knows how to handle and harmonize breath, body, and mind in this way.

Walking Meditation and Strong Emotions

Walking meditation can also be a wonderful way to work with strong emotions that may come up at work such as anger, resentment, or frustration. Practicing staying with your mindful breathing and mindful steps requires you to acknowledge these emotions, instead of rushing past them or suppressing them. There is a way to transform our suffering and free ourselves from it. If we rush past, we'll just be ignoring our suffering rather than finding true relief from it. In order to find the way out of our suffering, we must first accept it and look deeply to understand its true nature and origin. Once we've begun this work within ourselves, we can bring our understanding into our work environment, and use it to help not only ourselves but also the people around us with whom we work. So if strong emotions come up in us at work, like anger or frustration, we can stop what we're doing immediately and take care of the emotions. If anger arises, don't say or do anything. This is very important. Go out immediately and practice walking meditation and mindful breathing. Stop all thinking and just focus on your steps and your breath. You'll see that your emotions will gradually calm.

If you're a manager or a supervisor, you probably know that trying to enforce rules from a place of anger and violence, using your authority to control or suppress your coworkers, doesn't bring peace, happiness, or harmony. It's the same with strong emotions, whether they are your own or those of others. If you try to ignore your feelings or if you try to force yourself to think or feel something different, you won't succeed. Walking meditation is a way to remind ourselves to accept our feelings, to be with what is, rather than pushing on and pretending it isn't there.

Dealing with Anger

Suppose you have a difficult relationship with one of your coworkers. You and your coworker are angry with each other over a perceived slight, a promotion, or an occasion when the other person didn't listen to you or acknowledge you. You may blame everything on the other person. You think that that you're the only one who's suffering, that the other person isn't suffering at all. And you believe you're not responsible for your suffering, that it's the other person's fault. But you are co-responsible for the difficulty in the relationship. A relationship is between two people who, like all of us, are connected to each other. The other person's part of the misunderstanding that has arisen between you cannot exist without your part. Both are responsible for creating the situation.

We can transform our thinking by practicing mindfulness. When you practice mindfulness, you become more aware of yourself. When anger comes up, you know anger is there. So you practice mindful breathing and you say: "Breathing in, I know anger is in me. Breathing out, I will take good care of my anger." If you practice according to this teaching, you won't be reactive, you won't be tempted to immediately say or do something to the person with whom you are angry. Saying or doing something in anger will only be destructive. Don't say anything. Don't react. Just continue to practice mindful breathing and mindful walking. Embrace your anger, recognize it, and bring relief to your anger. After that, you can look deeply into your anger and ask yourself why you are angry.

When your room is too cold, you turn on the radiator and it begins to send out waves of warm air. The warm air doesn't try to fight the cold air. It comes and embraces the cold air, and five or ten minutes later the cold air has become warmer. In the same way, the energy of mindfulness and concentration embraces the energy of pain or anger.

Maybe the seed of anger within you is large. As soon as we hear or see something that isn't pleasant, the seed of anger within us is watered, and we become angry. We are the primary cause of our suffering, not someone else. The other person is just a secondary cause. If we know that, we are less angry. If we look deeply into our anger, we see that it has been caused by misunderstanding, wrong perceptions, and wrong views. Once we have realized this, our anger becomes transformed and understanding arises.

Restoring Good Communication at Work

We have to make a commitment to ourselves, and to our community at work, that from now on, every time anger manifests, we won't do anything or say anything until we've calmed down. We might like to use a "Peace Treaty," to remind us of this commitment. According to this practice, we need to look deeply into ourselves in order to recognize the roots of our anger. But if we're not able to transform it, then we have to go to the person with whom we're angry and ask for their help so we can correct our wrong perceptions. This should be done only after we have tried dealing with our anger on our own first, but not so long afterward that the anger has had time to solidify. Usually, it's best to communicate our need for help within twenty-four hours, because it's not healthy to keep anger inside if we can't resolve it.

Let the other person know that you're angry, that you're suffering because of it, and that you don't know why they said or did the thing that upset you. Ask for help and an explanation. If you're so angry that you can't tell him or her directly, write it down and give it to them.

Here are three sentences you may find very useful.

The first sentence is: "Dear colleague or friend: I am suffering. I am angry. I want you to know it." Because your lives are connected, you have the duty to tell the other person what you're feeling.

The second sentence you may like to write down is: "I am doing my best." This means that I am practicing mindful breathing, I have refrained from saying things and doing things out of anger and instead I am looking deeply and trying to practice right thought and right speech. That second sentence will inspire a lot of respect in the other person, and he or she will try to practice also.

The third sentence is: "Please help me." You may want to elaborate and say, "I cannot deal with this anger alone. I have practiced. But almost twenty-four hours have passed, and I haven't found much relief. I can't transform it alone. Please help me."

Asking for help is a wonderful thing. Usually, when we get hurt, we're inclined to say: "I don't need you. I don't need your help. I can survive all alone." And you get even more angry. If you can bring yourself to write "Please help me," then your anger will subside right away. Instead of trying to cope on your own, say the opposite: "I need you. I'm suffering. Please come and help."

If you want more happiness in your work life, memorize these three sentences. You may like to write them down on a piece of paper and slip it into your wallet as a bell of mindfulness. Every time anger comes up, the first thing you can do before reacting, before saying or doing anything, is take out your wallet and read these three sentences.

Practicing the Peace Treaty

A Peace Treaty can help us calm down and ease difficulties with people at work. We can read this regularly to remind ourselves of what to do in case we get angry with someone, or in case someone is angry with us.

The main thing to remember is not to say or do anything when we get angry, but to come back to our breathing immediately. Following our breathing, we can calm down. We can speak to the other person about what has made us angry. But first we need to look deeply into ourselves to see that the real cause of our anger is actually the strong seed of anger within us. The other person is only a secondary cause of our anger.

If we feel we've hurt someone else or made them angry, we can apologize right away, because we know that our own happiness depends on their happiness, and the suffering of others becomes our own suffering. With this awareness, we try to restore communication and our relationships with others as soon as possible.

The following text is adapted from the Plum Village Peace Treaty, originally designed to help couples resolve their conflicts, improve communication, and maintain a good relationship. You may like to discuss this slightly adapted version with your colleagues at work and hang it in a place where everyone can read it regularly, to remind yourselves of what to do should a difficulty with a colleague at work arise, and so that each person can better understand and accept their own responsibility in the conflict.

Peace Treaty

In order that we may work happily together, and that we may deepen our understanding of each other, we, the workers in _____
_____ (this team / office / department / company / etc. . .) vow to observe and practice the following:

I, the one who is angry, agree to:

1. Refrain from saying or doing anything that might cause further damage or escalate the anger.
2. Not suppress my anger.
3. Practice breathing and taking refuge in the island of myself.
4. Calmly, within twenty-four hours, tell the one who has made me angry about my anger and suffering, either verbally or by delivering a Peace Note.
5. Ask for an appointment later in the week, e.g., on Friday, either verbally or by sending a note, to discuss this matter more thoroughly.
6. Not say, "I am not angry, it's OK. I am not suffering. There is nothing to be angry about, at least not enough to make me angry."
7. Practice breathing and looking into my daily life in order to see:
   a. The ways that I, myself, have been unskillful at times.
   b. How I have hurt the other person because of my own negative or unskillful habit energy.
   c. How the strong seed of anger in me is the primary cause of my anger.
   d. How the other person's suffering, which has watered the seed of my anger, is only the secondary cause.
   e. How the other person is only seeking relief from his or her suffering.
   f. That as long as the other person suffers, I cannot be truly happy.

8. Apologize immediately, without waiting for the appointed meeting day, as soon as I recognize my unskillfulness and lack of mindfulness.
9. Postpone the meeting if I do not feel calm enough to meet with the other person.

I, the one who has made the other angry, agree to:

1. Respect the other person's feelings, not ridicule him or her and allow enough time for him or her to calm down.
2. Not press for an immediate discussion.
3. Confirm the other person's request for a meeting, either verbally or by note, and assure them that I will be there.
4. If I can apologize, do so right away and not wait until the appointed time of meeting.
5. Practice breathing and taking refuge in the island of myself to see how:
   a. I have seeds of anger and unkindness as well as the habit energy to make the other person unhappy.
   b. I have mistakenly thought that making the other person suffer would relieve my own suffering.
   c. By making him/her suffer, I make myself suffer.
6. Apologize as soon as I realize my unskillfulness and lack of mindfulness without making any attempt to justify myself and without waiting for the appointed meeting.

We the workers in this _____
(department) are determined to practice wholeheartedly to restore communication, mutual understanding, and harmony amongst ourselves whenever difficulties arise.

Signed, the _____ day of _____, in the year_____, at_____.

Riding the Storm

When a mental formation like a strong emotion arises, we say to it, "You are only an emotion." An emotion is something that comes, stays for some time, and finally goes away.

Our person is made of our body, feelings, perceptions, mental formations, and consciousness. The territory is large. You are much more than just one emotion. This is the insight you gain when a strong emotion comes up. "Hello my emotion. I know you are there. I will take care of you." You practice deep, mindful, abdominal breathing, and you know that you can handle the storm that has arisen in you. You can sit down in the lotus position or some other comfortable position on the ground, or lie down. Put your hand on your stomach, and breathe in very deeply, breathe out very deeply, and become aware of the rising and falling of your abdomen. Stop all thinking. Just be aware of your breath and the movement in your body. "Breathing in, my abdomen is rising. Breathing out, my abdomen is falling." Completely concentrate on the rising and falling of your abdomen. Stop all thinking, because the more you think about what has upset you, the stronger your emotion will become.

While practicing like this, don't allow yourself to stay at the level of your thinking. Bring your awareness down to the level of your breathing, just below the navel. Just become aware of the rising and falling of your abdomen. Stick to this, and you will be safe. It's like a tree in a storm: when you look at the top of the tree, you see the branches and leaves swaying violently back and forth in the wind. You may have the impression that the tree is going to break or be blown away. But when you bring your attention down to the trunk of the tree, you see how stable it is and you know that the tree is deeply and firmly rooted in the earth and can't be blown away. You know that the tree is going to withstand the storm. So when you're engulfed in the storm of strong emotions, don't dwell at the top of the tree, at the level of thinking. Stop the thinking. Go down to the trunk, to your abdomen. Embrace the trunk and focus one hundred percent of your attention on the rise and fall of the abdomen. As long as you maintain mindful breathing, and focus solely on the rising and falling of your abdomen, you will be safe.

Don't wait until a strong emotion arises to begin this practice of mindful breathing or you will forget what to do when you need it most. We have to begin to practice right now, while the sky is clear and there are no storms on the horizon. If we practice for five or ten minutes every day, we'll naturally remember how to practice when we most need it, and we can survive the onslaught of a strong emotion very easily.

Your Thoughts, Speech, and Actions Bear Your Signature

Suppose you have a colleague with whom you work with often and with whom you want to maintain good relations. There are a few things you may like to do. The first thing is to notice the way you think about your work and your work relationships.

Your work may involve offering a service to others or producing an object or commodity that you may think is the purpose of your work. But while at work, you are also producing something else: thoughts, speech, and actions.

When a composer or a painter creates a work of art, they always sign it. In your daily life, your thoughts, speech, and actions also bear your signature. If your thinking is right thinking, containing understanding, compassion, and insight, it's a good work of art, and it bears your signature. If you can produce a thought that is compassionate and insightful, that is your creation, your legacy. It's not possible for it not to bear your mark because it's your creation.

Everything you say is a product of who you are and how you think. Whether your speech is kind or cruel, it bears your signature. What you say may cause a lot of anger, despair, and pessimism, and that, too, bears your signature. It's not good to produce such negativity. With mindfulness, you can produce speech that contains understanding, compassion, joy, and forgiveness.

When you have enough peace and happiness within you, then whatever you say will transmit these positive elements to other people and will help water the good seeds in them, allowing the positive elements in them to grow. They, in turn, will know how to water what is positive in the people they talk to. If talking is only for the purpose of complaining about other people at work, expressing your anger, frustration, and violence, then you will do harm to yourself and to others. Mindful conversation is a good practice. When we speak, we should be aware of the effect that our conversation will have on others.

Loving Speech

Using loving speech means speaking with love, compassion, and understanding. We try not to use words of blaming or criticizing. We try not to speak with judgment, bitterness, or anger because we know that such words can create a lot of suffering. We speak calmly, with understanding, using only words that inspire confidence, joy, and hope in others.

Loving speech invites other people to express themselves

and their difficulties. We must be honest, we must be open, and we must also be ready to listen. When we listen deeply with compassion, we understand what kind of wrong perceptions others may have about us, or even about themselves. Equally, by listening deeply we may recognize that we, too, have wrong perceptions about ourselves and about other people. Communication helps both sides to remove wrong perceptions and to have a clearer view of the other, a view that is closer to the truth.

Even if we use loving speech, some people may respond with cynicism and suspicion because they've had negative experiences in the past. They don't trust others easily. They haven't received enough love and understanding. They suspect that what we offer them isn't authentic love, authentic compassion. Even if we really do have love and understanding to offer, they're still suspicious or skeptical. There are many young people who haven't received sufficient understanding and love from their families, their parents, their teachers, or society. They don't see anything beautiful, true, or good in the world around them. So they wander around, seeking something to believe in, craving love and understanding. They wander around like hungry ghosts, never satisfied.

In the Buddhist tradition, a hungry ghost is a spirit with a big belly who is always hungry. Although their bellies have plenty of room, they can't eat much because they only have a narrow throat, the size of a needle, so their capacity to swallow food is very small. Due to having such tiny throats, they can never eat their fill; they're never satiated. We can use this image to describe the way people are when they are hungry for love and understanding, and yet their capacity to receive love and understanding is very small. You have to help bring the size of their throat back to normal before they can swallow the food that you offer. That is the practice of patience, continued loving kindness, and understanding. It takes time to win their trust. Until that time, you can't help them. That's why, even if faced with cynicism, skepticism, or mistrust on the part of others, you have to continue with your practice undeterred.

Every one of us, whether we're psychotherapists, judges, lawyers, teachers, police officers, scientists, artists, or computer programmers, can try to apply these practices of deep listening and loving speech in order to improve communication in the workplace. When good communication is established, everything is possible. Communication helps remove wrong perceptions and misunderstandings.

Deep Listening

Deep listening simply means listening with compassion. Even if the other person is full of wrong perceptions, discrimination, blaming, judging, and criticizing, you are still capable of sitting quietly and listening, without interrupting, without reacting. Because you know that if you can listen like that, the other person will feel enormous relief. You remember that you are listening with only one purpose in mind: to give the other person a chance to express themselves, because up until now no one has taken the time to listen. Now you are a bodhisattva of listening. This is a practice of compassion. If you can keep compassion alive in you while listening, you won't become irritated. Compassion protects you from getting irritated or angry when you hear things that are unjust, full of blaming, bitterness, or recrimination. It's wonderful. You can keep compassion alive in you because you know that by listening like this, you give someone a chance to express themselves and to feel understood. It's so simple.

You keep breathing in and out and maintain awareness. If you practice like this, you can listen for a long time without the seed of anger in you being touched.

If at some point you feel that the anger or irritation is beginning to arise, then you know that your capacity for compassionate listening is not strong enough. Nevertheless, you can still practice loving speech. You can say: "I think I'm not in very good form today. Can we continue some other time, maybe the day after tomorrow?" Don't make too much effort. If your quality of listening is not good, then the other person will know it, so don't try too hard.

When you speak, you have the right to share everything in your heart, provided that you use loving speech. However, while speaking, a block of pain or anger in you may come up, and it may be heard in your voice. In that case you know that your capacity for loving speech is not good enough and you can say: "Would you give me a chance to speak another time? Today I'm not at my best." And you take a few more days to practice mindful breathing, mindful walking, and calming down so that you can practice loving speech the next time you speak.

Mindful Meetings

Meetings can often be a source of tension, stress, and conflict, so in Plum Village we have certain practices to help us maintain peace and harmony during meetings.

Before we start a meeting, we sit quietly and come back to ourselves. We listen to the sound of the bell to help us come back to our breathing and the present moment, calming our body and mind, and letting go of worries. Then we read a text to remind us to use loving speech and deep listening—to honor, respect, and be open to the views of others and to practice nonattachment to our own views. We know that the harmony of the community is the most important element for our collective happiness and that if we are attached to our present views, or try to impose them on others, we will create suffering. So we practice being open and listening to the experience and insight of others. We invite everybody to express their ideas and we come to a consensus after we've heard everybody's views. We know that the collective wisdom and insight of the Sangha is greater than the wisdom of any one individual. If we can't reach a consensus, we agree to discuss the matter again at a later time.

During the meeting, we practice using loving speech and deep listening. We let one person speak at a time; we never interrupt. While one person is speaking, the others all practice deep listening, trying to understand what the person wants to say. Deep listening means listening attentively to hear what the other person is saying and what is being left unsaid. We practice listening without judging or reacting. We don't get caught up in verbal duels. We speak from our own experience and address the whole group and if we have questions, we place the question in the center of the circle for the whole group to contemplate and address. You might find it helpful to read the following text before you start a meeting or adapt it to suit your needs.

Meditation before a Meeting

We vow to go through this meeting in a spirit of togetherness as we review all ideas and consolidate them into a harmonious understanding—a consensus. We vow to use methods of loving speech and deep listening in order to bring about the success of this meeting. We vow not to hesitate to share our ideas and insights but also vow not to say anything when the feeling of irritation is present in us. We are resolutely determined not to allow tension to build up in this meeting. If anyone senses the start of tension, we will stop immediately and come back to our breathing straight away, in order to reestablish the atmosphere of togetherness and harmony.

We also have times when we sit together in a meeting but we don't talk about work. We have a weekly meeting called a "happiness meeting," which might last about an hour, but we don't speak about work at all—we just remind each other that we have more than enough conditions of happiness already available to us; we don't need to look for more conditions of happiness in the future. Sitting together reminds us that we are very lucky. We might drink a cup of tea and nourish each other with our presence and the practice of mindfulness. We might share a story about a positive experience that we've had recently. We water the seeds of happiness in everyone and enjoy each other's presence. We see the positive qualities in the others and we express our gratitude. We feel very happy and very lucky to be able to sit together.

Sitting together like this and enjoying each other's presence is possible in any kind of workplace. Many of these practices can be applied to the life of a business or company.

CHAPTER FOUR

coming home

I Have Arrived, I Am Home

When we get home from work, we're often full of stress and tension from the day. Our bodies are suffering because we've worked them too hard—we haven't taken good enough care of them. The body has absorbed many toxins from the things we've consumed and due to the way we eat, drink, work, and overwork. We might like to look at the state we're in when we get home and think about how we can release the tension and toxins in the body.

Suppose you work late at night. You may wonder, "Why do I have to be here so late when everyone else is either out enjoying themselves or at home sleeping?" Thinking about your work like this can make it become very difficult. If you continue, you may find yourself feeling resentful, depleted of energy and nourishment. After work, you go straight home to sleep because you're so tired. If you live with others, this exhaustion can take a heavy toll on your relationships and on your family life. But if you know the practice of mindfulness you'll be able to transform your long working hours into a positive and nourishing experience.

When you enter Plum Village, there's a sign that says, "I have arrived. I am home." You may choose to put a sign like this on your front door as well, as a gentle reminder that you don't have to run after anything else anymore. You don't just come home to sleep and go back out again, but to enjoy being at home, to enjoy being with your family or those you live with, and to restore and nourish yourself. When you come home, you can take the time to arrive, to be fully there for yourself and for those around you.

Coming Home to Ourselves

If you're working a lot and feel stressed, there's probably a lack of communication in yourself—between your body and your mind. Your body and your consciousness may have been trying to tell you something for a long time, but you may have been too busy to listen properly.

Many of us have not had enough practice in listening to our bodies. The first step each of us must take when we want to return home is to bring attention to ourselves and notice what's going on with our emotions and in our bodies. The body is our first home. We can't feel at home in the outside world if we're not at home in our own bodies.

What keeps us from being at home? Often, our inner home doesn't feel comfortable—it feels too messy, full of difficult feelings, and we want to avoid spending time there. But we need to come home to ourselves in order to take care of these feelings. We don't need to have resolved everything before we come home. Even if you just have the awareness of the present moment and the intention to return to your body, this is more than good enough; you are already a part-time Buddha. Maybe you have transformed only one or two percent of the suffering within you, yet you can be happy because you have now seen a path.

The second step is to practice with your family and those closest to you. You don't need to wait until you've transformed all of your suffering in order to be able to help your family. Use loving speech and listen deeply in communication with your parents, your partner, and your children. If possible, invite them to join you on the path of transformation and healing, because your family should be the foundation of support for your practice. Without the support of your family, your partner, your children, it's more difficult to be mindful yourself.

You can become an active member of your family through the practice of coming home. There are families in which nobody feels that it's a real family; there's no solid foundation. It's like a hotel where people simply come and go, coming home only to sleep; everyone has his or her own life; there's no communication or mutual support. The practice of returning home to ourselves will help us rebuild the family and turn it into a living organism. When there's enough awareness, transformation, and joy within the family, both you and your family will become a source of strength and support for the wider community.

Being Present

Many of us try to divide ourselves up because we feel we don't have enough time. We imagine we give eighty percent of ourselves to our work, ten percent to our family, five percent to our friends and two percent to do charitable work. But if you do this, you end up never being fully present anywhere for anyone. Wherever you are, you can be there one hundred percent. You can be fully present.

Gardeners can't garden unless they're physically present in the garden, taking care of the different flowers, the trees, the vegetables, and the greens. If there are flowers that have wilted or branches that have broken off, or if there are weeds, grass, or fallen leaves, then a good gardener knows how to transform this decaying vegetable matter and can turn it into rich compost to nourish the trees and the flowers. Our body, our feelings, our perceptions, our mind, and our consciousness are our garden and we need to be fully present to work in our garden, just like the gardener who is watering, weeding, and transforming.

We need to be present for ourselves. Imagine a country without a government, without a president, a king, or a queen. That country would have nobody to take care of it. Every country needs to have some form of government. It's the same for ourselves. We need to be present in our own "country," to take care of ourselves, to be the king, the queen, or the president. We need to know what is precious and beautiful in order to protect it, just as we need to know what is not beautiful in order to remove it or fix it. We need to be there and not run away from our responsibility. There are, however, people who don't want to be the king; they don't want to take on this responsibility, they just want to run away because it's so tiring being the king.

We use many means to run away. We run away by watching television, by reading the newspaper, we go on the internet, we play computer games, or we listen to music. We don't want to return to our land. We are kings or queens who refuse to accept the responsibility of governing our own state. But we need to become aware of our responsibility; we need to take on the role of governor, return home, and take care of ourselves.

Part of taking good care of ourselves is knowing that we have limitations and we can't do everything. Our bodies and our energy are limited. As a teacher, I also have limits. I would like to be able to travel everywhere and teach in all the places I'm invited to. But if I allowed myself to do that, in spite of my desire to help as many people as possible, I would die sooner from exhaustion because the demand is very great and my body and health are limited. We have to learn to say no in order to preserve ourselves, so we can continue our life and work longer.

You have to acknowledge the fact that you have your limits. You have more than enough intelligence to be able to know your limits and to adopt a working schedule that responds to your true needs, for your own good and for the good of your family and your community.

A Breathing Room

Just as you need a place at work to breathe in, like a quiet room, a part of your office, or even just a corner of your desk, at home you also need a breathing room—a quiet, calm place where you can enjoy your breathing and come back to yourself, a space in which you can nourish yourself and cultivate joy. You might like to set up a little table with some flowers and a candle and enjoy sitting there alone or together with the members of your family.

When you come home, you may have a lot of housework or other chores to do, but it's important to take a few moments first to just sit and breathe. This will restore you and allow you to do whatever tasks you have to do with more freshness, awareness, and joy.

Sitting Together

In the time of the Buddha, hundreds of monks came to visit him to receive teachings. They sometimes arrived late at night and one of the Buddha's attendants would invite them in to come and sit with the Buddha and his Sangha. Sometimes, students of the Buddha would walk a whole month before arriving in the place where the Buddha was staying. They had no telephone to announce that they were coming so they often arrived unexpectedly. One time, hundreds of these travelling monks came and sat peacefully with the Buddha until midnight. At midnight, Ananda, the Buddha's attendant, stepped very lightly over to the Buddha and said gently, "Lord Buddha, it's twelve o'clock. Would you like to teach the monks something?" The Buddha didn't say anything—he just continued to sit. Ananda went back to his place and sat down. At two in the morning, Ananda got up again, came to the Buddha lightly, and said, "World-Honored One, it's two in the morning. Would you like to teach us something now? You can go ahead and teach." Again, the Buddha continued to sit quietly and didn't say anything. Ananda went and sat back in his place until five in the morning. At five o'clock he stood up and, with soft footsteps, went one more time to the Buddha, "It's five o'clock in the morning. Do you want to say anything; do you want to teach anything?" Finally the Buddha looked at Ananda and asked, "Ananda, what do you want me to talk about? Isn't it enough that we can just sit together? That's enough happiness. What do we need to say?"

Sitting together is enough to bring us happiness. When we sit with full awareness, we are really there in the present moment. We have really come home; we have truly arrived. If you have a time and a place reserved for sitting peacefully and quietly like this in your home, you will find that you'll look forward to going home.

Housework

When we get home from work, often all we want to do is rest. We look on the things that have to be done around the house as more work, such as cooking, tidying up and cleaning, and we don't want to do any additional work if we've already worked the whole day. But if we have time to relax and restore ourselves, to renew our energy, then we can see these things as bringing us joy rather than adding to our workload or our feeling of stress.

Although just sitting is indeed wonderful, we don't have to sit in order to be happy. We can be happy mopping the floor. Imagine if you didn't have a home. There are many people who don't have a home to clean. But you do. You feel very happy that you have a floor to mop. Cooking, sweeping, vacuuming, and cleaning can bring us so much happiness.

There are people who think, "How can I possibly be happy cleaning the toilet?" But we're lucky to have a toilet to clean. When I was a novice monk in Vietnam, we didn't have toilets. I lived in a temple with one hundred people and no toilet. Yet we managed to survive. Around the temple there were bushes and hills so we just went up on the hill. They didn't have rolls of toilet paper up on the hill—you had to take dry banana leaves or hope to find some leaves out on the hill. When I was a child at home, before becoming a monk, we didn't have a toilet either. Only a very few people were rich enough to have toilets. Everybody else had to go into the rice fields or up on the hill. At that time, there were twenty-five million people in Vietnam, most of them without toilets. Having a toilet to clean at all is enough to make us happy.

Every bit of work we do at home can be an opportunity to practice awareness and gratitude like this. Doing the cooking becomes a source of happiness because we're aware that we have a kitchen, we have a stove, and we have food to cook, food to nourish us.

Perhaps one of the reasons we don't enjoy all these activities as much as we could is because we think activities need to be exciting for us to enjoy them. Many people confuse joy and happiness with excitement. But excitement is not the same as happiness. With joy and happiness we have a sense of satisfaction. There's a feeling of satisfaction in being in the here and now, when you recognize you have so many conditions for happiness in the present moment, whether you're sitting, walking, standing, or working. If you can recognize this, you can generate a feeling of happiness at any time. You can remind others with your mindfulness. Perhaps they will begin to enjoy cooking and cleaning as well. These activities become even more enjoyable when we can do them together.

CHAPTER FIVE

a new way
of working

ACCORDING TO THE TRADITIONAL BUSINESS MODEL in many Western countries, competition is the only way to achieve success. We think we're powerful when we're at our most competitive and believe we can only be successful if others fail. But when someone wins, someone else will lose and will suffer. That is competition. We compare ourselves to others: "I'm better than you." This kind of thinking can only reinforce the mind of discrimination and our complexes of superiority, inferiority, or equality. When we lose, we suffer because we think this means that someone else is better than we are. Yet if we look deeply, we see that this thinking is based on a false discrimination between self and other. If we continue thinking in this way, we'll go in the direction of self-destruction.

It is very clear that in competition there can be no winner. Those striving to be the best, to be at the top, have to work very hard to get there, and doing this, they suffer a lot. Once they reach the top, they have to keep on striving in order to stay there, and often they suffer from enormous stress and become burnt out. If we continue living like this, we're heading not only toward self-destruction but also toward the destruction of our planet. That's why we need to wake up; we need a huge collective awakening to change the course of our civilization or we'll destroy each other, our loved ones, and the Earth's natural resources. In this competition there can be no winner. Everyone will lose. Discriminating between self and other causes a lot of suffering. The wisdom of nondiscrimination and the insight of interbeing can help us to understand that you are in me and I am in you.

When I was ordained as a novice monk, my teacher showed me how to bow to the Buddha. We recited a verse: "The one who bows and the one who is bowed to are both by nature empty." This means empty of a separate self. We should not be proud. I am made of non-me elements, including you. And you are made up of non-you elements, including me. So if you compete with other beings, you are also competing with yourself.

This doesn't mean, though, that we're all alike. When we look at something like a flower, although we're looking at the same thing, the way we see the flower may be different. Everyone has a different way of seeing. We shouldn't try to make people think the same way we do or do things in the same way as we would. What we want is that the thinking is productive, that it brings about more understanding and more compassion, and that they have more peace. We all want more joy, peace, and freedom. The way we produce these wonderful things may be different, but we don't need to compete with each other to get them. We can only get them if we work together, in our different ways, as part of a whole.

The Three Powers

Many of us think that if we had a lot of power we could do whatever we wanted, and that this would make us very happy. Indeed, many of us have some kind of power, but because we don't know how to handle the power, we misuse it and we create suffering for ourselves and for the people around us. Money is a kind of power. Fame is a kind of power. Weapons are a kind of power. A strong army is a kind of power. A lot of suffering is caused in the world because people misuse their power. They do this because they don't have the power to be themselves.

In the Buddhist tradition, we speak of three powers. These are quite different than the power of fame, wealth, and competition. These three kinds of power can make a person happy. If you have these three kinds of power, then the other kinds of power like having money, fame, an army, or weapons will never become destructive.

The First Power: Understanding

The first kind of power is the power of understanding. We should be able to cultivate the power to understand our own suffering and the suffering of others. This kind of understanding will bring about compassion that will reduce our own suffering. When you understand, you are no longer angry; you no longer want to punish anyone. Understanding is a great power. It gives rise to compassion.

When you have sufficient understanding, you release all your fear, anger, and despair. Understanding means understanding the roots of suffering in yourself, in others, and in the world. We use the energy of mindfulness and concentration to look deeply into the nature of our suffering in order to gain understanding. In Buddhism, we don't speak of salvation in terms of grace. We speak of salvation in terms of understanding. Understanding is a like a sword that can cut through the afflictions of anger, fear, and despair.

The Second Power: Love

If you put a handful of salt into a bowl of water and stir it, the water will be too salty to drink. But if you throw the same amount of salt into an immense river, the handful of salt can't make the river salty. The power of love is like the river. If your heart grows, your heart has room for everyone. When your heart is full of love, little irritations become like the handful of salt in the river. They don't bother you, and you don't suffer anymore.

The energy of love can free you and also help free the people around you who suffer. There are two ways to respond to difficulties you have with others. In the first way, you have the desire to punish the person you believe has made you suffer. You believe that you are a victim of someone else and you have the tendency to want to punish that person because he or she has dared to make you suffer. You may feel tempted to retaliate and to punish them. But of course when the other person is punished, he or she suffers and wants to retaliate and punish you back. This is how the situation escalates. Yet there's another way to respond. You can respond to suffering with the power of love. When you look deeply, you realize that the person who has made you suffer also suffers very deeply. He suffers a lot from his wrong perceptions, his anger, or his fear. He doesn't know how to handle the suffering in himself. If no one offers love and understanding, he becomes the victim of his own suffering. If you look deeply with the eyes of love and see this, compassion will be born in your heart. When compassion is born in your heart, you don't suffer anymore, and you ease the suffering of others.

The Third Power: Letting Go

The third power is the power to be able to detach and let go of our afflictions, such as craving, anger, fear, and despair. When you have the power to cut away all these kinds of afflictions, you become a free person and there is no greater power than that. When you're free, you can help so many people to suffer less.

We all have the energy of craving within us, but we can cultivate the power of being able to cut through this kind of energy. We know that the object of our craving has brought us a lot of suffering and has brought other people around us a lot of suffering, too. Mindfulness, concentration, and understanding give us the power to overcome our attachment to our afflictions.

In the beginning, you believe that the objects of your craving are essential for your well-being and happiness. You let your cravings have power over you. But if you look deeply, you will recognize that these objects of craving are not true conditions for your happiness. If you can see this, and you can cultivate the powers of love and understanding, then you'll be truly powerful.

The Three Powers in Business

Other kinds of power—money, fame, sex, and wealth—can turn you into a victim and cause you to hurt others. But the three powers of love, understanding, and letting go can never make you suffer and will never make other people suffer either. These three real powers can only make you happy and help create happiness for others as well. Whatever your profession, every day provides an opportunity for you to cultivate the power to understand suffering; the power to accept, to love, and to forgive; and the power to cut off and transform your afflictions.

Suppose you're a business leader. You want to succeed in your business. If you know how to cultivate these three kinds of power, you'll never misuse the power you have in your hands, whether money, fame, or other kinds of resources. You'll no longer want to punish, or destroy. You'll know how to conduct your business in a way that protects the environment and all living beings. You won't misuse the kind of power that is available to you now.

If you want to practice with the three powers and still be a financially successful business, the first thing you need to do is to go back to yourself. If you want to go far and realize your dreams, you need to learn how to take care of yourself first of all. We should all learn the art of mindful breathing and mindful walking to bring our mind back to our body. With the practice of mindfulness, we can free ourselves from worry and fear concerning the future, and from regret and sorrow concerning the past. With the energy of mindfulness and concentration we can listen to our own suffering and transform it.

Only when we can establish harmony, love, and happiness within ourselves are we in a position to really help our business. There may be a lot of misunderstanding, frustration, and anger in the company. Directors, employers, and employees may be suffering. If you're not happy within yourself, if you're not feeling light enough, you can't run your business, company, or corporation happily and successfully. If you've cultivated the powers of compassion and understanding, you can listen to everyone in the company with compassion, love, and understanding and help your employees to suffer less. Part of being a good business leader is having the time to sit and listen to others. When someone feels that you have understood them and you support them, they become your ally, and not only a worker. The time you spend listening to everyone in the business is not lost time. This time turns your company into something much more than a business—something wonderful that can be very nourishing for you and for all the employees.

Balancing Happiness and Profit: Four Business Models

I think it's possible for businesses, companies, or corporations to focus more on happiness and well-being and not only on profit. In Plum Village, we focus on happiness. That's why we have a lot of time to take care of ourselves, and we need this time because we know that unless we take good care of ourselves we can't take good care of other people. If we didn't focus on happiness, if we only focused on profit, suffering would result.

Focusing only on happiness is one way to run a business, but a business also needs to have a source of income or some other way of sustaining itself. So we can run a business by placing a lot of emphasis on happiness, but by placing some emphasis on profit as well. A third model focuses solely on profit, and there is no happiness. Finally, in some businesses, there is no happiness, and there is no profit either. This kind of business won't last long! Our business can make a lot of profit, but we shouldn't sacrifice happiness for it. We don't want to be in a business that makes a lot of profit but has no happiness at all. If we focus on making profit like this, we destroy ourselves, the environment, our happiness, and the happiness of other living beings. However, if we focus on the three powers of understanding, love, and letting go, then happiness will follow. Profit may result as well, but never at the cost of happiness.

A New Work Ethic

As an individual, you may have your own code of behavior to live by. Similarly, your family or your workplace may have agreed upon some kinds of practice or a code of ethics to guide them as a family or a community. Maybe you all agree to sit together quietly before meals at home or before meetings at work. Maybe you all agree that if you're angry, you'll sit down quietly and calmly before talking with the other person. These mutual agreements can protect and nourish you, your family, and those with whom you work.

For a workplace to function well, there must be a code of behavior that everyone is willing to accept. Although your job may be to supervise people at work, it doesn't mean you can give orders or create rules and then force people to follow them. This won't work. If you engage in a power struggle with others, you can never unite happily as an organism, as a community. You won't have a happy or harmonious work atmosphere. As a teacher, I don't use my authority to force my students to do what I want them to do. Using authority doesn't work. Instead, I sit down with my students and try to help them see that their negative speech, behavior, or actions aren't bringing happiness, either to themselves or to the community.

Understanding is the very foundation of love. If you don't understand others' difficulties, pain, suffering, and deepest aspirations, you can't truly take good care of them or make them happy. This is why understanding is love. Do you take the time to look deeply and to understand the roots of your own suffering, your own pain and sorrow? Are you capable of treating yourself with compassion? If not, how can you relate to others with understanding and compassion? Developing compassion and understanding can promote a code of behavior that will make your workplace harmonious, happy, and peaceful.

When you start a new job, you become part of an existing work culture. That work culture may be respectful of other people and their ideas or it may be disrespectful. Perhaps nobody feels responsible for their own work culture, that it just is what it is and can't be changed. In fact this isn't true. Mindfulness gives us the opportunity to think about how we want to work together with other people and how to create a workplace code of ethics. Once we see each other as human beings, we can realize we have shared goals, hopes, and ethics.

Practicing The Five Mindfulness Trainings

In Plum Village, we've come up with the Five Mindfulness Trainings, which represent our vision for a global spirituality and ethic. They're not based on the commandments of any religion, but rather on an understanding of what will bring us all mutual health and happiness. The Five Mindfulness Trainings are very relevant in today's working world—they can serve as the basis for your company's work ethic. Following these guidelines, you can contribute not only to your own personal happiness and well-being, but also to the happiness and well-being of the people at work and all those you deal with, which in turn will have a beneficial effect on the whole world.

The first mindfulness training is to preserve and protect life. The second training is the practice of true happiness—the kind of happiness that won't destroy you or the environment. The third training is about true love. True love is the kind of love that creates only joy and happiness. The fourth mindfulness training is the practice of deep listening and loving speech in order to restore communication. The fifth mindfulness training is the practice of mindful consumption. We practice consuming in a way that preserves ourselves, all species, and our planet.

The Five Mindfulness Trainings

Reverence for Life

The First Mindfulness Training

Aware of the suffering caused by the destruction of life, I am committed to cultivating the insight of interbeing and compassion and learning ways to protect the lives of people, animals, plants, and minerals. I am determined not to kill, not to let others kill, and not to support any act of killing in the world, in my thinking, or in my way of life. Seeing that harmful actions arise from anger, fear, greed, and intolerance, which in turn come from dualistic and discriminative thinking, I will cultivate openness, nondiscrimination, and nonattachment to views in order to transform violence, fanaticism, and dogmatism in myself and in the world.

True Happiness

The Second Mindfulness Training

Aware of the suffering caused by exploitation, social injustice, stealing, and oppression, I am committed to practicing generosity in my thinking, speaking, and acting. I am determined not to steal and not to possess anything that should belong to others; and I will share my time, energy, and material resources with those who are in need. I will practice looking deeply to see that the happiness and suffering of others are not separate from my own happiness and suffering; that true happiness is not possible without understanding and compassion; and that running after wealth, fame, power and sensual pleasures can bring much suffering and despair. I am aware that happiness depends on my mental attitude and not on external conditions, and that I can live happily in the present moment simply by remembering that I already have more than enough conditions to be happy. I am committed to practicing Right Livelihood so that I can help reduce the suffering of living beings on Earth and reverse the process of global warming.

True Love
The Third Mindfulness Training

Aware of the suffering caused by sexual misconduct, I am committed to cultivating responsibility and learning ways to protect the safety and integrity of individuals, couples, families, and society. Knowing that sexual desire is not love, and that sexual activity motivated by craving always harms myself as well as others, I am determined not to engage in sexual relations without true love and a deep, long-term commitment made known to my family and friends. I will do everything in my power to protect children from sexual abuse and to prevent couples and families from being broken by sexual misconduct. Seeing that body and mind are one, I am committed to learning appropriate ways to take care of my sexual energy and cultivating loving kindness, compassion, joy and inclusiveness—which are the four basic elements of true love—for my greater happiness and the greater happiness of others. Practicing true love, we know that we will continue beautifully into the future.

Loving Speech and Deep Listening
The Fourth Mindfulness Training

Aware of the suffering caused by unmindful speech and the inability to listen to others, I am committed to cultivating loving speech and compassionate listening in order to relieve suffering and to promote reconciliation and peace in myself and among other people, ethnic and religious groups, and nations. Knowing that words can create happiness or suffering, I am committed to speaking truthfully using words that inspire confidence, joy, and hope. When anger is manifesting in me, I am determined not to speak. I will practice mindful breathing and walking in order to recognize and to look deeply into my anger. I know that the roots of anger can be found in my wrong perceptions and lack of understanding of the suffering in myself and in the other person. I will speak and listen in a way that can help myself and the other person to transform suffering and see the way out of difficult situations. I am determined not to spread news that I do not know to be certain and not to utter words that can cause division or discord. I will practice Right Diligence to nourish my capacity for understanding, love, joy, and inclusiveness, and gradually transform anger, violence, and fear that lie deep in my consciousness.

Nourishment and Healing

The Fifth Mindfulness Training

Aware of the suffering caused by unmindful consumption, I am committed to cultivating good health, both physical and mental, for myself, my family, and my society by practicing mindful eating, drinking, and consuming. I will practice looking deeply into how I consume the Four Kinds of Nutriments, namely edible foods, sense impressions, volition, and consciousness. I am determined not to gamble, or to use alcohol, drugs, or any other products which contain toxins, such as certain websites, electronic games, TV programs, films, magazines, books, and conversations. I will practice coming back to the present moment to be in touch with the refreshing, healing, and nourishing elements in me and around me, not letting regrets and sorrow drag me back into the past nor letting anxieties, fear, or craving pull me out of the present moment. I am determined not to try to cover up loneliness, anxiety, or other suffering by losing myself in consumption. I will contemplate interbeing and consume in a way that preserves peace, joy, and well-being in my body and consciousness, and in the collective body and consciousness of my family, my society and the Earth.

Your workplace, school, business, or company could choose to adopt the Five Mindfulness Trainings as the basis of your work ethic. You can also decide to follow these trainings as an individual or as a family. The trainings are all based on the insight of interbeing. Interbeing means that nothing can exist on its own. Everything is with everything else; everything is in everything else. Everything inter-is. You exist with everything else, you inter-are with everything else.

Suppose we look deeply at a rose. With some concentration and mindfulness, we can see that the rose is made of only non-rose elements. What do we see in the rose? We see a cloud, because we know that without the cloud, there would be no rain, and without the rain, the rose couldn't grow. So a cloud is a non-rose element that we can recognize if we look deeply into the rose. Next, we can see sunshine, which is also crucial for the rose to grow. The sunshine is another non-rose element present in the rose. If you took the sunshine and the cloud out of the rose, there would be no rose left. If we continue like this, we see many other non-rose elements within the rose, including the minerals, the soil, the farmer, the gardener, and so on. The whole cosmos has come together in order to produce the wonder we call a rose. A rose cannot be by herself alone. A rose has to inter-be with the whole cosmos. That is the insight we call interbeing.

Happiness is also a kind of rose. Happiness is made exclusively of non-happiness elements. If you try to throw away all the non-happiness elements—like suffering, pain, worry, despair—you will never have happiness. Similarly, when you grow lotus flowers, you need mud. Looking deeply into the lotus flower, you can see the mud. You can't grow a lotus on marble. A lotus is made only of non-lotus elements—like mud—just as happiness is made of non-happiness elements. That is the nature of interbeing. Everything is inside everything else. We can't try to keep one thing and get rid of the other thing because they're in each other.

Happiness is not an individual matter. One person's happiness, if it is true happiness, will have an effect on other people, just as a tree can have a beneficial effect on the world around it. If a tree is healthy, upright, and beautiful, even if the tree doesn't do anything, the fact that it is there, healthy and beautiful, can benefit the whole world. The same is true with people. If someone is happy, their happiness can benefit everyone around them. This is why I think of happiness as a workplace matter. Our happiness affects our work and those around us. We're not separate from each other.

Whatever your job is, it may be helpful to spend some time as a group reflecting on how to bring about true happiness at work. We need to ask ourselves the question, "What is true happiness?" When there's no sense of community, of working together in harmony for the good of all, then there's also no happiness, even if you have a lot of power or a lot of money. When we understand this, we can reflect, as a group of people who work together, how to carry out our work and how to conduct our business so that real happiness, love, and peace are possible in our daily lives.

We Have Enough

Perhaps you have a job that you enjoy, but you find the people you work with difficult. Or it may be that you feel the work you do is neither beneficial for yourself, nor for others or for the environment, but you have a good reason why you need to continue this job, at least for the time being. Whatever your situation, you can already have happiness at work, right now. You don't need to wait for the future. Your mindful breathing, awareness of your steps, and a growing community of practice can help create that happiness.

We tend to believe that we don't have enough conditions of happiness in our lives for us to be happy. We have a tendency to run into the future to look for more conditions of happiness. But if we go home to the here and the now and, with mindfulness, recognize the conditions of happiness and joy that already exist, we find that we have more than enough to be happy and joyful right now.

If you're not aware of the sunshine, you always live in the dark. Mindfulness helps you to see that there is sunshine! How wonderful. There are rolling hills. There are birds. There are trees. Our planet is beautiful. Mindfulness helps me realize I have a body. I am alive. I can see. I have lungs and I can breathe. My feet and legs are strong enough for me to walk and run. There are so many conditions of happiness. If we tried to write down all the conditions of happiness that we already have, one page wouldn't be enough, two pages wouldn't be enough, ten pages wouldn't be enough. We have more than enough to be happy.

Three Methods for Nourishing Happiness

There are many ways we can nourish our happiness, at home and at work. The first method for nourishing happiness is to look and see that in our bodies and all around us we already have many conditions of happiness. Our eyes are bright, our ears can hear, our bodies still work. Around us there is air that we can breathe, a beautiful sky—we just need to be truly present in the here and now to see all this. Recognizing the many conditions for happiness we already have is one way we can create happiness.

The second method for creating happiness is to compare our current situation with situations of unhappiness in the past. We've all experienced moments when we had difficulties or suffered deeply, for example, when a loved one died, or when we, or someone we love, had a serious accident or illness. At such times, we had so much suffering that it was very difficult for us to feel or create happiness. Although these things happened in the past, the memories remain; we keep the images alive inside us. If we call these images up now and compare them with the present moment, we can see very clearly that our present situation is much better. With this awareness, happiness arises right away.

If we take a notebook with a blue cover, for example, and we put a smaller, white piece of paper on top of it, then we see the contrast of colors. The blue notebook represents our past suffering and the white piece of paper is our current happiness. When we compare the two we see the difference very clearly, and the white suddenly looks much whiter—whiter than white. In comparison to our past suffering, we can see the precious conditions of happiness we have right now. Comparing past and present situations makes our happiness shine more brightly.

The third method of nourishing happiness is to stay focused on the present moment and practice the art of living with both joy and suffering, accepting and embracing our suffering and not fighting or repressing it. When we've had a lot of suffering in our past, it can become a habit to hold on to the suffering, the pain, and the difficulties. But we can remind ourselves not to live in that past. If suffering arises, either because we're thinking about the past or because of real suffering in the present, we don't need to cling on to it. We can use mindfulness to acknowledge our suffering and say to it, "I know you are there, and I am here for you." Just saying this, our suffering lessens. Our suffering is embraced and calmed and suddenly there is space for joy. We need to embrace our suffering tenderly, like a mother embracing and comforting her crying baby. When the mother is fully attentive to the crying baby, the baby calms down. Don't fight or struggle with your suffering, just recognize and embrace it, and joy and happiness can arise.

With these three methods for nourishing happiness, we know that happiness is possible, even at work. We can let go of our worries and our minds become clearer and lighter. We can focus on our intentions for the day. We're not trapped by fear, anger, or suffering, and we can move toward our desire to do our jobs well, to do good work that benefits both ourselves and the planet.

Right Livelihood

The Buddha spoke about Right Livelihood as one of the eight factors leading to happiness. How do we know if we're practicing Right Livelihood? To practice Right Livelihood means to engage in work that nurtures our ideal of compassion and understanding. We try to make choices that bring about the most benefit and cause the least amount of harm to ourselves and others, as well as to animals, plants, and the entire planet. Even if this means having a job that brings us less money than we might otherwise be able to earn, it can produce much happiness. Right Livelihood is a question of ethics and how to produce well-being, not only for ourselves but for all those affected by our work—directly or indirectly.

The way you live your life, the work you do, and the way you work, contribute to a collective awakening of others and to society as a whole. We need a collective awakening for a future on Earth to be possible. You can ask yourself how your work helps others. If you're motivated by the desire to help others, you'll have so much more joy and energy for your work. Nothing can compare to the joy of knowing that life on Earth and your contribution to it is beautiful and helpful.

It's important to know how to nourish our happiness,

and the kind of work we choose to do is an important factor. So many of our modern industries are harmful to humans and nature; it's very difficult to practice right livelihood. If we don't look carefully at what we're doing, we can cause a lot of harm. The production of food is a good example. If someone works in commercial farming, he or she may feel they are benefiting others by helping grow food for people to eat. But if the farm they're working on uses chemical poisons, working there may actually be harming humans and the environment. If a farmer tries to respect the environment by refusing to use such chemicals, it may be difficult to compete commercially, and it can be a struggle to survive financially. If the farmer does succeed in running an organic farm profitably, it may still be difficult to grow truly healthy food as long as the neighboring farms are still using pesticides and chemical fertilizers, which pollute the air, soil, and water. We're all connected and our work has far-reaching effects. Right livelihood is not a purely personal matter. Our work choices don't only affect ourselves, our families, and loved ones; our work choices affect the choices and the health of our neighbors and of those around the globe.

The Spiritual Dimension of Work

A gentleman who drove a very luxurious car once came to see me. He told me he was responsible for designing nuclear warheads. His conscience was very troubled by doing such work, but he felt responsible for supporting his family financially and didn't think he could quit his job. Despite the potentially destructive work he was doing, this engineer had a conscience. He was aware of what he was doing. The world needs mindful people like this working in such jobs. If this man were to resign, another less mindful person with less awareness of the potential negative consequences of his work might replace him, which would be worse. However, if he were to find a way to get people to stop doing this kind of work altogether, that would be best of all. If no one were willing to design nuclear warheads, they wouldn't continue to be manufactured or used. Our engineer knew that if he wanted to enjoy a sense of peace brought about by practicing right livelihood, he wouldn't be able to continue in his current job for the rest of his life; he would need to find another kind of work and take steps to go in that direction.

However demanding our jobs, whether we're social workers, police officers, emergency room doctors, designers, software engineers, scientists, or teachers, we can all become bodhisattvas, carrying out our work with understanding and awareness. The lawyer can practice looking deeply with compassion and understanding, and turn being a lawyer into a vocation in which understanding and reconciliation are cultivated, which brings about healing, rather than focusing on conflict and confrontation. A lawyer can see his or her job as helping clients look deeply so that transformation, reconciliation, and healing become possible. Of course, the lawyer has to represent her client and argue her case well; but she can also speak her heart and share her insights to help her client understand the other side's point of view. When a lawyer expresses herself in court, she can water the seeds of understanding and compassion in the hearts of everyone, including the judge. This is very important. That kind of practice will be noticed and appreciated by many people.

A mindful politician can also act according to his conscience and independent insight. He's capable of voting mindfully, possibly at odds with his own party. By showing honesty and good will, other members of his party will understand him and he'll enjoy the support of the people. So it's very important to bring the dimension of practice, a spiritual dimension, into your work. We need people like that in our world.

Co-Responsibility

No matter what work you do, you actually represent all of us; you are doing it in our name. We are co-responsible for your acts and we will all suffer if you do work that isn't good, either for living beings or for the planet as a whole. If you feel you need to continue in a job that is not nourishing, you can still do it mindfully. If you continue to practice mindfulness, you will eventually gain more insight, which will help you either to improve your current work situation or to leave your job and find a new, more nourishing one. Become aware of your compassion and cultivate it. Don't become a machine, running on automatic pilot— remain a human being and keep your compassion alive.

Suppose I'm a schoolteacher and I find joy in my work, nurturing love and understanding in children. I would object if someone were to ask me to stop teaching and become a butcher, for example. However, when I meditate on the interrelatedness of all things, I can see that the butcher is not the only person responsible for killing animals. He does his work for all of us who eat meat. We are co-responsible for his act of killing. We may think the butcher's livelihood is wrong and ours is right, but if we didn't eat meat, he wouldn't have to kill, or he would kill fewer animals. Right livelihood is a collective matter. The livelihood of each person affects us all, and vice versa. The butcher's children may benefit from my teaching on respecting and preserving life, while my children, if they eat meat, share some responsibility for the effects of the butcher's choice of livelihood.

Any look at right livelihood entails more than just examining the situation in which we earn our paycheck. Our whole life and our whole society are intrinsically linked. Everything we do contributes to our effort to practice right livelihood, and we can never succeed one hundred percent until we all go in the right direction together. But each of us can resolve to go in the direction of compassion, in the direction of reducing suffering in the world. Each of us can resolve to work for a society in which there is more understanding, love, and compassion.

Millions of people, for example, make their living working in the arms industry, helping directly or indirectly to manufacture both "conventional" and nuclear weapons. The U.S., Russia, France, Britain, China, and Germany are the primary suppliers of these weapons. So-called conventional weapons are then sold to poorer countries, where the people don't need guns, tanks, or bombs; they need food. To manufacture or sell weapons is not right livelihood, but the responsibility for this situation lies with all of us—politicians, economists, and consumers. We all share responsibility for the death and destruction that these weapons cause. If you're able to work in a profession that helps you realize your ideal of compassion, please be grateful. Please try to help create proper jobs for others by living mindfully, simply, and sanely.

Because there is such a culture of exploitation and destruction of the Earth, it's a challenge to find work that one can support wholeheartedly, that one can really stand behind and morally agree with. It takes time, a firm intention, and a deep aspiration. Don't despair or give up if you're not yet in a position where you feel you can practice right livelihood one hundred percent. You can go in the direction of right livelihood and do the work that you currently do with mindfulness and compassion. Whatever job you have right now, whether it's your true calling or just a temporary situation until you can find something better, you can always find a way to create more well-being at work.

A Collective Awakening

Regardless of what work we do, part of our work is to help bring about a collective healing, transformation, and awakening for our own well-being and for the sake of our planet. The insight of interbeing can help in this, but we need a collective awakening. Every one of us has to work to produce this collective awakening. If you're a journalist, you can do this as a journalist. If you're a teacher, you can do this as a teacher. Without this awakening, nothing will change. Awakening and awareness are the foundation of all change. Each of us has to sit down and look deeply to see what we can be, what we can do today to help relieve the suffering around us, to help reduce stress, and to bring about more joy and happiness. We can do this by ourselves or with a group of people, with our colleagues or with our family. There is so much suffering in the world but, at the same time, there is also the potential for so much joy. By living your life with awareness, producing your own work of art, you can contribute to the work of collective awakening.

Every human being has the capacity for understanding and love. Everyone has the seed of great love inside. There's a Buddhist story about a bodhisattva whose name was Never Disparaging. His only job was to go around telling people, "I don't dare to underestimate you. You have the capacity to become a Buddha, a person with great awareness and compassion." That was his only message. He made a vow to go to everyone—rich, poor, educated, less educated—and he always said the same thing. Sometimes people thought that he was making fun of them. Sometimes they beat him up. But he still continued, "This is what I truly believe. I want to bring you the message that you are capable of becoming a Buddha. Everyone is capable of understanding and of loving."

But one Buddha is not enough, we need others, even if they're only part-time buddhas. When we live our lives with awareness, we'll naturally, and without effort, transform the lives of those around us. We can start by building a collective community of practitioners that can support us when we go through hard times. The collective energy of mindfulness is very powerful. When we surround ourselves with people who are also practicing mindfulness, we benefit from their energy. It's like allowing the water in the stream to be embraced by the ocean.

Creating Community at Work

Once you've tried practicing mindfulness at work for a while, you can see if there are others who would be interested in practicing mindful breathing, sitting, and walking with you. If you're surrounded by people who are practicing mindfulness together, then you'll all be supported by the collective energy, and the practice will become very easy, very natural.

Even if at first you can't find others in the same workplace to practice with you, your practice will nevertheless have a beneficial effect on those around you and on the whole work environment. The more you practice mindfulness, the more you will know how to change your work environment in a positive way. Every one of us is capable of contributing to the collective energy of mindfulness. Your practice of mindful breathing and mindful walking will support the others around you. When we practice mindful breathing and mindful walking, we become a bell of mindfulness for everyone. When you walk mindfully, enjoying every step you make, you encourage others to do the same, even if they don't know that you're practicing mindfulness. When you smile, your smile supports everyone around you and you remind others to smile as well. The presence you have when you practice is very important.

When you're on your own and you don't have the collective energy of your community, you still have to practice in order to protect yourself from the strong emotions, violence, and anger of others. And you also have to practice to protect yourself from accidents, from your own unskillfulness, and your own anger. If you spill something, trip, injure yourself, or explode in anger at someone, these are all accidents that come from not practicing enough mindfulness. If you're peaceful and lucid, you won't attract accidents.

Everyone Needs a Sangha

We all have difficulties at work sometimes. We all have pain, sorrow, and fear within. But we don't need to keep it to ourselves—we can find a community to practice with and allow the community to embrace it for us. None of us is strong enough to embrace our pain and sorrow alone.

When you throw a rock into a river, no matter how small the rock is, it will sink to the bottom of the river. But if you have a boat, you can carry many tons of rocks and they won't sink. The same is true with our suffering: our sorrow, fear, worries, and pain are like rocks that can be carried. If we allow the community and the collective energy of mindfulness to embrace us, then we won't sink in the ocean of suffering. Our pain and suffering become lighter. We can practice mindfulness alone, yes, but it's much easier and more supportive to have a community to practice with. When many people practice mindfulness together, the collective energy is much stronger and this helps us do the work of transformation and healing that we all need. Without this collective energy, we're likely to lose sight of our practice and eventually abandon it. If you want your practice to continue, you should create a group of people around you who practice together, and your practice will be sustained by the collective energy of the group.

If we know we're making steps in the right direction, that's good enough. The goal is not to be perfect in everything we do, but to make steady progress on the path. If you're in a situation or a job that requires you to continue living in a way that goes against the spirit of right livelihood, then you could consider it temporary until you can find a different, less stressful job that will allow you to live a simpler and happier life, without harming humans or nature.

Meanwhile there are things you can do. You can practice mindfulness each day and cultivate compassion within yourself. You can introduce secular mindfulness practices to your workplace. Having a good job is important. But being honest, living peacefully, and having a path to follow is more important. No matter what work you do, mindfulness can help you follow a path that leads to right livelihood and a life of more joy, happiness, compassion, and understanding. If we can work in a way that encourages this kind of thinking and acting, a future will be possible for ourselves, our children, their children, and for the entire planet.

CHAPTER SIX

thirty ways to reduce stress at work

Start your day with ten minutes of sitting meditation.

✦

Remind yourself of your gratitude at being alive and having twenty-four brand-new hours to live.

✦

Take the time to eat breakfast at home. Sit down and enjoy it.

✦

At the end of the day, keep a journal of all the good things that happened in your day. Water your seeds of joy and gratitude regularly so they can grow.

✦

Take the stairs at work instead of the elevator and go up them in mindfulness, combining each step with your breathing.

✦

Use the time waiting at the bus stop or train station as an opportunity to practice sitting meditation or slow walking meditation, following your breathing and enjoying having nowhere to go and nothing to do.

✦

Turn off your cell phone while in the car, on your way to work, or during breaks.

✦

Resist the urge to make calls on your cell phone while on your way to and from work or on your way to appointments. Allow yourself this time to just be with yourself, with nature, and the world around you.

✦

Use red traffic lights or traffic jams as bells of mindfulness inviting you to stop your thinking, slow down, and have a rest in the present moment. Become aware of any tension in the body while driving, or any irritation, anger or frustration and try to relax by coming back to your breathing. Relax your shoulders, face, and jaw. Don't try to change your breathing, just follow it.

✦

Arrange a breathing area at work where you can go to calm down, stop, and have a rest. If you don't have a particular area, you can arrange a corner of your desk with flowers and a little bell, which you can invite whenever you feel stressed. Take regular breathing breaks to come back to your body and to bring your thoughts back to the present moment.

Download a "mindfulness bell" onto your computer and program it to sound every fifteen minutes to remind you to have a breathing break and to stretch your body to release tension. A bell can be downloaded from: www.mindfulnessdc.org/mindfulclock.html.

✦

Instead of rushing to answer the phone when it rings, breathe in and out three times to make sure you're truly present for whoever is calling you. You may like to put your hand on the receiver while doing this to let your coworkers know you do in fact have the intention to pick up the phone; you're just not in a hurry.

✦

Make it a habit to do five to ten minutes of total relaxation every day in a corner of your office, or in a calm space at work where you can lie down, or in the park if it's sunny. Do a body scan and relax all the muscles in your body, sending love to all your organs and thanking them for the work they're doing all day long. This doesn't have to be long to be very rejuvenating. You'll feel much fresher, more peaceful, and restored after this, and your work will benefit.

✦

At lunchtime, eat only your food and not your fears or worries.

✦

If you wash up your dishes after the meal, or your coffee cup after a break, focus solely on the act of washing the dishes or the cup. You can recite the gatha for washing the dishes or make up your own. Bring your attention to the warm, soapy water, enjoy the time your hands are in the water, enjoy the act of cleaning your dishes or your coffee cup. Do this in silence, without talking, focusing all your attention on what you're doing and allowing yourself to enjoy this short break when you don't need to speak or do anything else. You can let your family or colleagues know that you don't want to be interrupted during this time and invite them to enjoy this practice as well. Just enjoy the present moment and the act of washing the dishes simply in order to wash the dishes.

✦

Make a ritual out of drinking your tea. Stop work and look deeply into your tea to see everything that went into making it: the clouds and the rain, the tea plantations and the workers harvesting the tea. Cultivate your gratitude by appreciating all the love and hard work that went into bringing your tea to you. Savor this moment of enjoying your tea.

✦

Leave your car at home one day a week and car pool, take public transport, or ride your bike to work. Enjoy your ride on the bus or the fresh air on your face as you cycle to work. Feel the strength of your body and your gratitude for having such a healthy body.

✦

Try not to divide your time into "my time" and "work time." All time can be your own time if you stay in the present moment and keep in touch with what's happening in your body and mind. There's no reason why your time at work should be any less pleasant than your time anywhere else.

✦

Change your work environment to make it a more peaceful and joyful environment by creating moments and spaces of calm, by working collaboratively with others, and by creating a sense of a working community.

✦

Before going to a meeting, visualize someone very peaceful, mindful, and skillful going with you to the meeting. Take refuge in this person—even if only an imaginary figure—to help you stay calm and peaceful during the meeting.

✦

If you feel strong emotions arising during a meeting, take a short break to go to the restroom and walk there in walking meditation. Enjoy your time in the restroom. Remember your time here is no less important than your work.

✦

If you feel anger or irritation arising at work, refrain from saying or doing anything. Come back to your breathing and follow your in- and out-breath until you've calmed down. Walking meditation can be helpful. Recognize your feelings. Say, "Hello my anger, my irritation. I know you are there. I will take good care of you."

✦

Practice looking at your boss, your superiors, your colleagues, or your subordinates as your allies and not as your enemies. Recognize that working collaboratively brings more satisfaction and joy than working alone. Wherever possible, work in a team. Know that the success and happiness of everyone is your own success and happiness.

✦

Try to relax and restore yourself before going home so you don't bring accumulated negative energy or frustration home with you. Walk home in mindfulness from the bus stop, or from wherever you've parked your car. Take some time to relax and come back to yourself when you get home before starting on household chores. Recognize that multitasking means you're never fully present for any one thing. Do one thing at a time and give it your full attention. Practice mono-tasking!

✦

Practice not working or talking and eating at the same time. Do one or the other in order to be fully present for your food, for your colleagues, or for your work.

✦

Don't eat lunch at your desk. Change environments. Go for a walk.

✦

Practice looking for the positive things in your work and in your colleagues. Express your gratitude and appreciation to them regularly for their positive qualities and good actions. This will transform the whole work environment, making it much more harmonious and pleasant for everyone.

✦

Start a meditation group at work and sit together a few times a week or join a local Sangha.

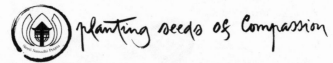
planting seeds of Compassion

If this book was helpful to you, please consider joining the Thich Nhat Hanh Continuation Fund today.

Your monthly gift will help more people discover mindfulness, and loving speech, which will reduce suffering in our world.

To join today, make a one-time gift or learn more, go to: www.ThichNhatHanhFoundation.org.

Or copy this form & send it to:
Thich Nhat Hanh Continuation and Legacy Foundation
2499 Melru Lane, Escondido, CA USA 92026

❏ Yes! I'll support Thich Nhat Hanh's work to increase mindfulness. I'll donate a monthly gift of:

   ❏ $10   ❏ $30($1 a day)   ❏ $50*   ❏ $100   ❏ $_____Other

Your monthly gift of $50 or more earns you a free sub to The Mindfulness Bell: a journal to the art of mindful living (US/Canada only).

❏ Please debit my bank account each month. I've enclosed a blank check marked "VOID".

❏ Please charge my credit card each month.

Your Name(s)_____

Name on Card/Account_____

Credit Card No._____ Exp. Date _____

Address_____

City_____ State/Prov_____ Zip/Postal_____

Country_____ Email_____

www.ThichNhatHanhFoundation.org
info@ThichNhatHanhFoundation.org

PARALLAX PRESS

Parallax Press, a nonprofit organization, publishes books on engaged Buddhism and the practice of mindfulness by Thich Nhat Hanh and other authors. All of Thich Nhat Hanh's work is available at our online store and in our free catalog. For a copy of the catalog, please contact:

Parallax Press
P.O. Box 7355
Berkeley, CA 94707
Tel: (510) 525-0101
www.parallax.org

Monastics and laypeople practice the art of mindful living in the tradition of Thich Nhat Hanh at retreat communities worldwide. To reach any of these communities, or for information about individuals and families joining for a practice period, please contact:

Plum Village
13 Martineau
33580 Dieulivol, France
www.plumvillage.org

Blue Cliff Monastery
3 Mindfulness Road
Pine Bush, NY 12566
www.bluecliffmonastery.org

Magnolia Grove Monastery
123 Towles Rd.
Batesville, MS 38606
www.magnoliagrovemonastery.org

Deer Park Monastery
2499 Melru Lane
Escondido, CA 92026
www.deerparkmonastery.org

The Mindfulness Bell, a journal of the art of mindful living in the tradition of Thich Nhat Hanh, is published three times a year by Plum Village. To subscribe or to see the worldwide directory of Sanghas, visit www.mindfulnessbell.org